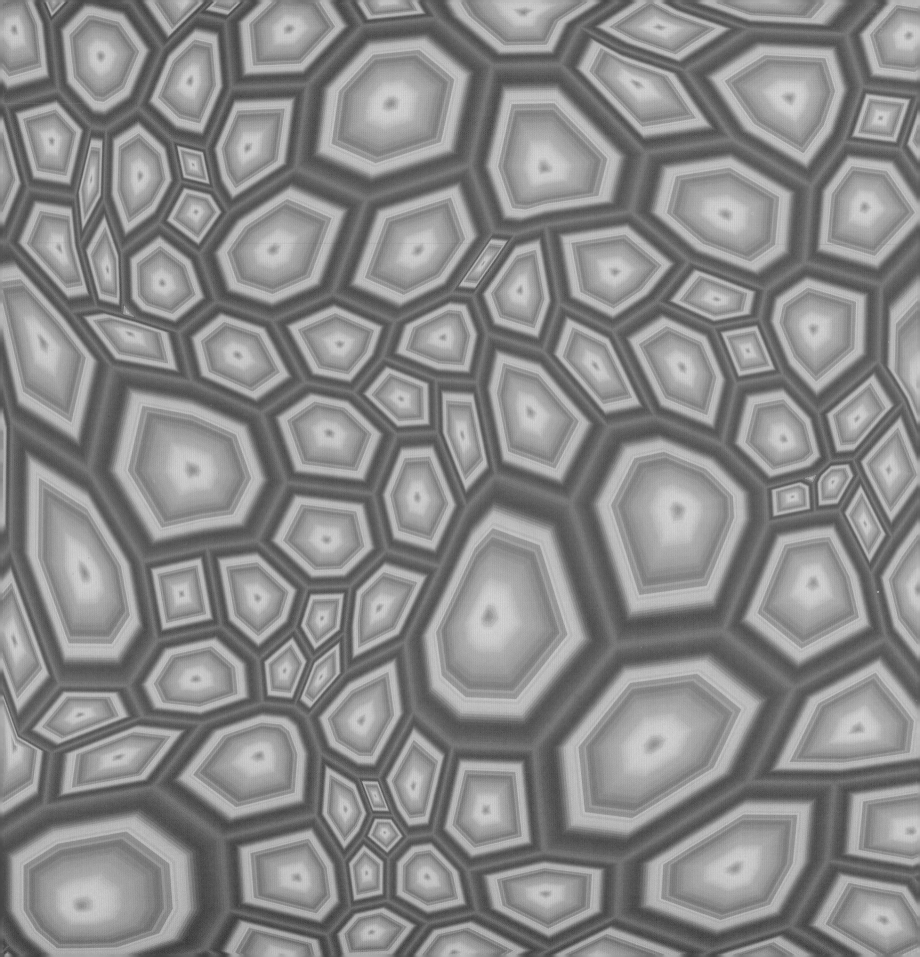

GRAPHICA 1: THE WORLD OF *MATHEMATICA*® GRAPHICS

THE IMAGINARY MADE REAL:
THE IMAGES OF MICHAEL TROTT

SERIES EDITOR AND CREATIVE DIRECTOR: JOHN BONADIES

WOLFRAM
MEDIA

Graphica 1: The World of Mathematica Graphics
The Imaginary Made Real: The Images of Michael Trott

Published by:

Wolfram Media, Inc.

100 Trade Center Drive

Champaign, IL 61820-7237, USA

email: info@wolfram-media.com

web: www.wolfram-media.com

ISBN: 1-57955-009-6

www.graphica.com

Distributed worldwide by:

A K Peters, Ltd.

63 South Avenue

Natick, Massachusetts 01760-4626, USA

email: service@akpeters.com

web: www.akpeters.com

ISBN: 1-56881-106-3

Credits:

Illustration: Michael Trott

Art/Creative direction: John Bonadies

Editorial: David Gehrig, Carrie Driscoll

Image preparation: Malgorzata Zawiślak

Publishing management: Allan Wylde

Production management: Judith Quinlan

Printed in China

INTRODUCTION

It seems so easy for nature to produce forms of great beauty—as so often imitated in art. But how does nature manage this? And must we be content with just imitating nature? Or can we perhaps capture whatever fundamental mechanism nature uses to produce the forms it does, and use this mechanism directly for ourselves?

My work in science has led me to the conclusion that for the first time in history, we are finally now at the point where this has become possible. And the key lies in the idea of computer programs. For a computer program, like a natural system, operates according to definite rules. And if we could capture those rules we should be able to make programs that do the kinds of things nature does.

But in fact we can do vastly more. For nature must follow the laws of our particular universe. Yet programs can follow whatever laws we choose. So we can in effect make an infinite collection of possible universes, not just our particular universe.

In the past, however, it has seemed difficult to get programs to yield anything like the kind of richness that we typically see in nature. And when one hears of images made by programs, one tends to think of rigid lines and simple geometrical figures. But what my work in science suggests is that people have created programs with too much purpose in mind: they have tried to make sure that their programs are set up to achieve specific goals that they can foresee.

But nature—so far as we know—has no goals. And so the programs it runs need not be chosen with any particular constraints. And what my work in science has shown is that programs picked almost at random will often produce behavior with just the kind of complexity—and sometimes beauty—that we see in nature. All that is necessary is that we go beyond the narrow kinds of programs whose behavior we, as humans, can readily foresee.

When I created *Mathematica* my goal was to build an environment in which one could easily set up programs of essentially any kind. And indeed the language that underlies *Mathematica* is based on concepts more general and more fundamental than even those of standard logic or mathematics. And by using these concepts it is possible to create programs that correspond to the kinds of rules that seem to operate in nature—or in anything like nature.

In fact, with the *Mathematica* language, remarkably simple programs can often produce pictures of such intricacy and unexpected detail that one would never imagine that they could ever have been made just by following any set of rules.

Sometimes the pictures one gets remind one of some familiar system in nature. And sometimes they look like the creations of a human artist. But often they are something different. They have parts reminiscent of nature. And parts that one could imagine being created by human artists. But then they have unexpected elements, like nothing seen before, together with a vast range of details far beyond what any unaided artist could ever produce.

And this is the essence of the images in *Graphica*.

—Stephen Wolfram
scientist and creator of *Mathematica*

WHAT IS *MATHEMATICA*? *Mathematica* is the tool used to create all of the images in this and other *Graphica* books. *Mathematica* is a software system—an environment for technical computing—originally designed by Stephen Wolfram as a tool for exploring ideas in science, technology, and elsewhere. *Mathematica* was first released in 1988, and in the years since that time it has become the tool of choice for well over a million scientists, engineers, financial analysts, students, and others. *Mathematica* has been used to design airplanes, to analyze stock markets, to manage fisheries, to discover important new science and mathematics, to solve innumerable homework exercises—and also to create art.

As its name suggests, *Mathematica* is built on mathematics, but mathematics interpreted in its broadest—and oldest—sense. *Mathematica* incorporates vastly more facts about algebra, trigonometry, calculus, and other fields of traditional mathematics than any human has ever known or probably ever will know. And it can use these facts to do in seconds calculations that would take humans months or years to do themselves. But the essence of *Mathematica* is its language.

It is not a language like English or French that has been built up haphazardly through centuries of use. It is a language that was designed from the start to provide a clear and precise way of communicating ideas—and a way that could be understood by a computer. Computer languages typically specify the operations in a rather literal and low-level way, most often giving quite explicit procedures for how data should be moved around inside the computer. But *Mathematica* is essentially unique among languages in common use in that it operates at a much higher level—with a much closer correspondence to normal human thinking.

All sorts of people use *Mathematica*, to do all sorts of things. Sometimes people use *Mathematica* like a calculator—asking it mathematical or other questions and letting it use its internal capabilities to work out the answer. Sometimes people use *Mathematica* like a notepad—to record and organize their thoughts and ideas. And sometimes people use *Mathematica* and its language to specify ways to create forms of all kinds—not just formulas and text, but also pictures and sounds. It is the implications of *Mathematica* as a tool for creating visual forms that the *Graphica* series explores.

MATHEMATICA BECOMES AN ARTIST'S TOOL With Wolfram Research's flagship product being based on higher mathematics, it might seem like an intimidating task for an art director to develop an effective visual communications identity. After all, mathematical imagery has traditionally been limited to stodgy charts, tables, and cryptic diagrams. But the graphics capabilities of *Mathematica* have instead allowed us to communicate our product and our company in a way that is both visually intriguing and distinctive.

Nor were we alone in using *Mathematica* to create interesting designs. A collection of graphic images included as a "Graphics Gallery" in the second edition of *The Mathematica Book* in 1991 inspired many users to take a closer look at *Mathematica*'s visualization tools. As a result, a proliferation of strange and interesting graphics began coming across my desk from all over the world.

And from the beginning, these images have not been only utilitarian or scientific. Many who use *Mathematica* in research or education have also come to use it as an artistic tool for their private enjoyment. There are also a growing number of creative people, without any formal training in science or math, who are beginning to experiment with *Mathematica* in their design work. And by now *Mathematica* has been used for set design, special effects in animation, textile design, sculpture, and architecture. And no doubt there are a host of other applications that we are yet to hear about.

Many times I have had the experience of showing these images to people who do not have a deep understanding of mathematics or science. And almost always their reaction has been a strange combination: initially an emotional, aesthetic response, followed by analytical curiosity. To our surprise and delight at Wolfram Research, this kind of reaction has been widespread in many communities.

The graphics in this volume demonstrate intricate connections between art, science, and mathematics that have been made possible by the advent of *Mathematica* as an artist's tool. I hope you find them as I did—unlike anything you have ever seen before. Their mixture of the familiar and the unknown, the algorithmic and the intuitive, has given me the exciting feeling of being present at the birth of a new art form.

—John Bonadies

 **UNVEILING THE BEAUTY OF MATHEMATICS** I use *Mathematica* every day, and I am always creating pictures. And over the past eight years, I have created roughly 6,000 such pictures. This book gives a small selection of these pictures.

The pictures were chosen and arranged by John Bonadies—guided purely by visual criteria. Sometimes all the pictures on a page will have technically been constructed in the same way, but more often they will have been constructed by quite different methods, and be united here purely for reasons for visual harmony.

Looking at all the images in this book, however, I can see that they also fall into another kind of creative classification—four groups each determined by a different underlying process of design.

 GROUP I The first group contains images for which I had a mental picture before sitting down at the computer. For these, I would take my inspiration from some form in nature, from previous graphics I have generated, or simply from whatever comes to mind when relaxing. Once I had a clear mental image of an object to be visualized, creating the image was generally a straightforward exercise in *Mathematica* programming—although one that, for the most intricate shapes, still took many hours.

Good examples of this approach to design are the hyperbolic dodecahedron (currently on the *Mathematica* box), a sphere covered with an Islamic decorative weave, and some of the three-dimensional flower-like structures.

After creating such basic surfaces, my next step was to make it more visually interesting—by changing colors and surface properties, by replacing plane polygons with three-dimensional sheets, by punching various kinds of holes into the polygons (or shrinking the existing ones to allow looking inside what had been a closed shape), by mapping patterns onto the surface, and by using a host of other such techniques.

Of course, changing colors to get better-looking graphics is often not such an easy task. Especially with a highly curved, self-intersecting surface, it can be quite difficult to arrive at a constellation of virtual light sources and surface color properties that will produce the desired colors. There were two approaches I took to this problem, one deterministic and the other probabilistic. In some cases, I performed direct calculations to discover the constellations of light sources and surface colors needed for the desired effect—sometimes a pretty complicated issue. In other cases, I would run the same picture a few dozen times overnight with randomly generated (within constraints) light positions, light colors, and surface color properties. In the morning, I would select the one I thought looked best—a sort of aesthetic counterpart of the "Monte Carlo" method. In some cases, I would reseed the random number generator at the beginning of each image so that the picture would be reproducible; in other cases I wouldn't, virtually guaranteeing that the same graphic will never be generated again.

 GROUP II That same capacity to generate random values can also be called into play in the creation of the objects themselves, as in the images of the second group. For examples, consider randomly generated mazes, a hexagonal Truchet pattern, or a densely packed arrangement of randomly worn stones. Although I had specified certain constraints when creating these images, by definition I could never know how the realizations would finally appear. In many cases, one can only imagine some limiting values—with no randomness or only a very small amount, perhaps, or completely unconstrained.

As a typical example, I would begin with a Platonic solid whose side faces have been divided into triangles. Next, I would rotate some randomly chosen individual triangles around the nearest edges, tracing out their paths to obtain a random arrangement of "bridges" and "tunnels" between the faces. For another example, imagine a plane covered with randomly chosen points in which each point is connected with its nearest neighbor. How will the resulting network look? Still another example would be a self-avoiding, closed random walk in three dimensions. The resulting shapes are in many cases quite unexpected and often interesting, too.

 GROUP III Mathematics and physics are rich sources for interesting images. The third group of pictures consists of visualizations of various mathematical functions, algorithms, and data. One could look at the pattern formed by the n-th digit in base b of a real-valued function of one variable on a rectangular grid; Chebychev polynomials $U_n(z)$ wrapped around circles; the values of a matrix representing an eigenvalue problem in certain special bases, represented as a density plot; multiple reflected light rays inside some closed concave curves; the partial sums formed by orthogonal polynomials dependent upon the argument; or moiré patterns of various lattices and grids with varying displacements and orientations. The possibilities are literally countless.

In such cases, all of the information describing the appearance of the final picture is already contained in the original function or algorithm, seed-like, but there is still a considerable amount of freedom of parameters to be chosen. Most functions and algorithms that one tries to visualize won't give a particularly intriguing picture or pattern, but from time to time quite pleasing ones will appear, worthy both of visualization and of a theoretical investigation of the mathematics underlying the structure. Also, in this category of "mainly determined functions" fall various topological surfaces such as the Klein bottle or Alexander's horned sphere. In such cases, most of the shape is mathematically determined, but there is still a considerable opportunity to select parameters to make the most attractive image.

 GROUP IV The fourth category contains images of well-defined and mathematically interesting or exceptional objects whose visualization is impossible without at least some analytical or numerical calculations. Can the reader of this book imagine without calculations the form of the surface $3-8x^2+8x^4-8y^2+8y^4-8z^2+8z^4$ in the x-y-z space? How about a faithful representation of the Riemann surface of the function $y(x)$ defined implicitly by $2x^5 - x^3 + x^4 - 2x^2 y - x y^2 + 2x y^4 + y^5 = 0$ via $\mathrm{Im}(y)(\mathrm{Re}(x),\mathrm{Im}(x))$?

In this kind of image, all of *Mathematica*'s symbolical and numerical capabilities come fully into play. One needs its symbolic capabilities to find appropriate parameterizations, to find symmetries and discretizations that reflect the underlying structure of these surfaces, and to calculate branch points by using resultants. One needs its numerical capabilities to solve corresponding systems of nonlinear differential equations and transform coordinates between various coordinate systems. Finally, one needs its graphical capabilities to render the surfaces under consideration. Having all these ingredients available in one system allows me to write a program, for example, to see the Riemann surface of an arbitrary algebraic equation of the form `Sum[a[i,j] x^i y^j,{i,0,n},{j,0,n}]` = 0, or the polyhedra representing the first 50 Brillioun zones of three-dimensional lattices.

As with the images in group three, many of the programs that are visualizations of mathematical functions and equations are in some sense completely deterministic. But of course one has a choice which polynomial or more general function to visualize. Thus, often in the evening I would choose some such function to explore, feed it into the Riemann surface generating program or some other tool, and in the morning look at the results. This procedure resulted in some of the most pleasant surprises.

Each of the four types of pictures described previously has its own challenges, enticements, and rewards. Pictures of the first two groups require more creativity, while those in the last two groups typically require more programming. The pictures from the last two groups, though, are fascinating to me. The form of the resulting picture is already nearly completely predetermined in the equation(s); one "only" has to unveil it into a picture.

This unveiling can, from time to time, require some nontrivial amount of coding. That I could produce so many images of such intricacy and mathematical accuracy is a reflection of *Mathematica*'s deep understanding of symbolic and numerical mathematics. Without *Mathematica*, this book would simply have been impossible to produce.

Images like these show, in a new way, some of the intrinsic beauty of the underlying mathematics itself, beauty that can be uncovered only by this kind of visualization. Readers interested in recreating pictures shown in this book or generating such pictures themselves should consult *The Mathematica Guidebook* (TELOS/Springer-Verlag, 1999). In that volume I give a detailed, self-contained description of the *Mathematica* programming involved in making interesting graphics, explain the underlying mathematics, and give recipes for creating similar pictures. Images from all four groups described above are included.

In their study of content, the aesthetic appearance of a function is not usually the concern of mathematicians. But in this book I have tried to unite rigorous substance with aesthetics, somewhat in the manner of art photographers who, given a fixed subject matter, use their artistic freedom to create the most interesting photographs.

A reflection of that duality of approach can be seen in a quote by the German mathematician, Karl Weierstrass (1815–1897). In German, the word *Darstellung* is used to mean "mathematical representation"; for example, the word for the power series representation of a function is *Reihendarstellung*. But *Darstellung* also carries the less rigorous meaning of "depiction."

With that ambiguity in mind, the spirit of this book can be encapsulated in Weierstrass' words:

"Das letzte Ziel ist immer die Darstellung einer Funktion."
"The final goal is always the representation/depiction of the function."

—Michael Trott

GALLERY

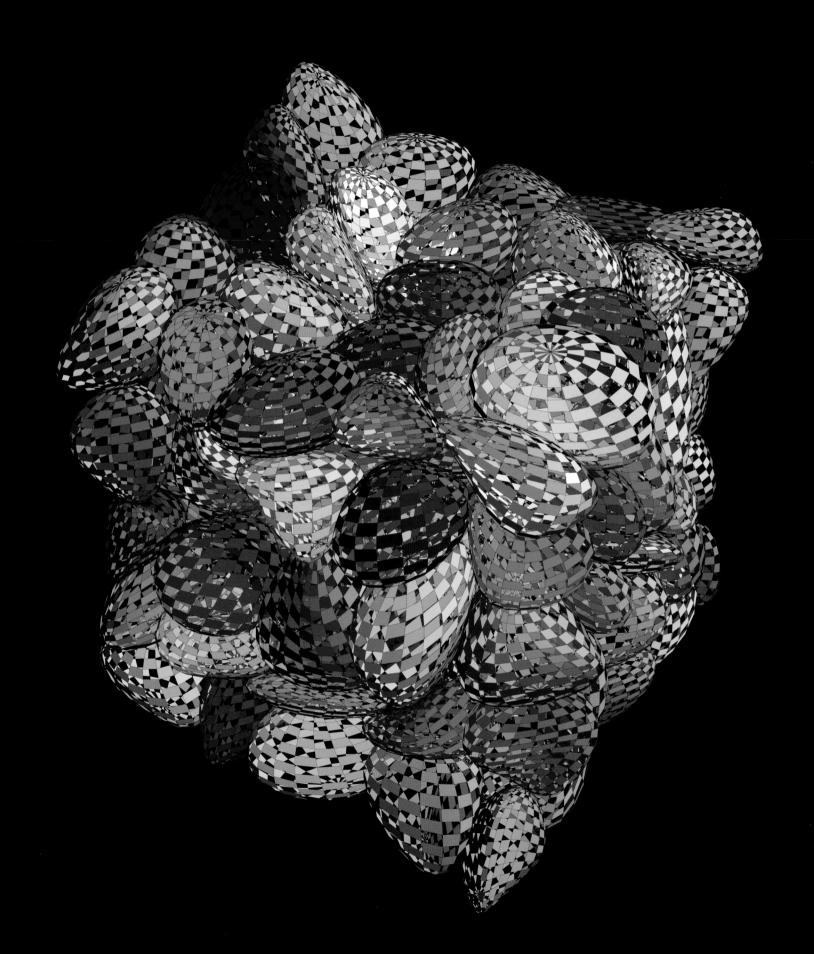

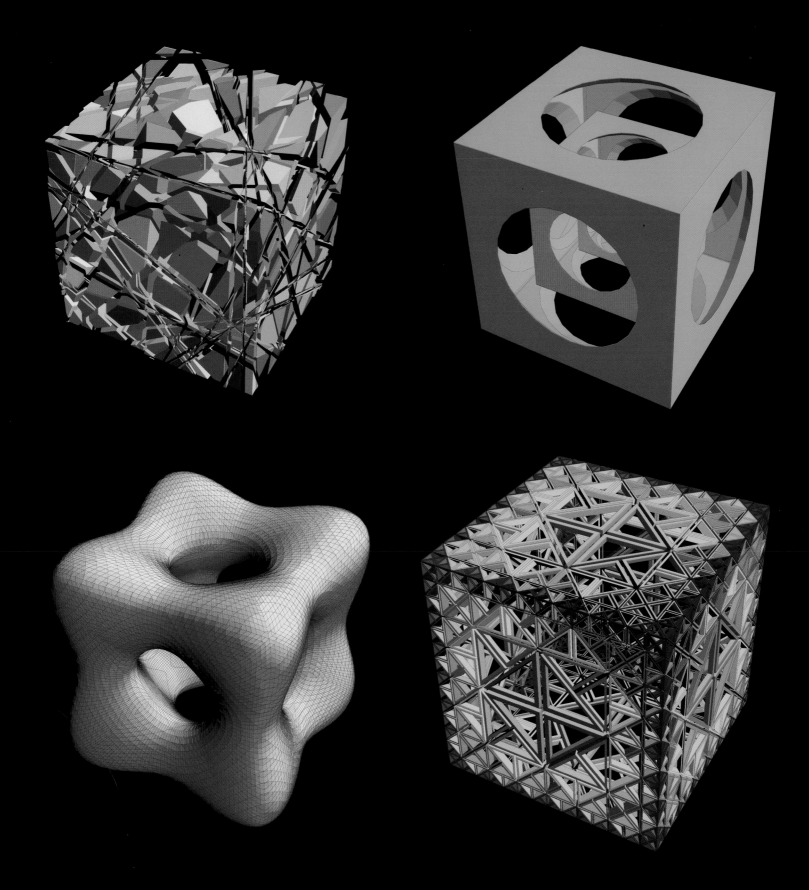

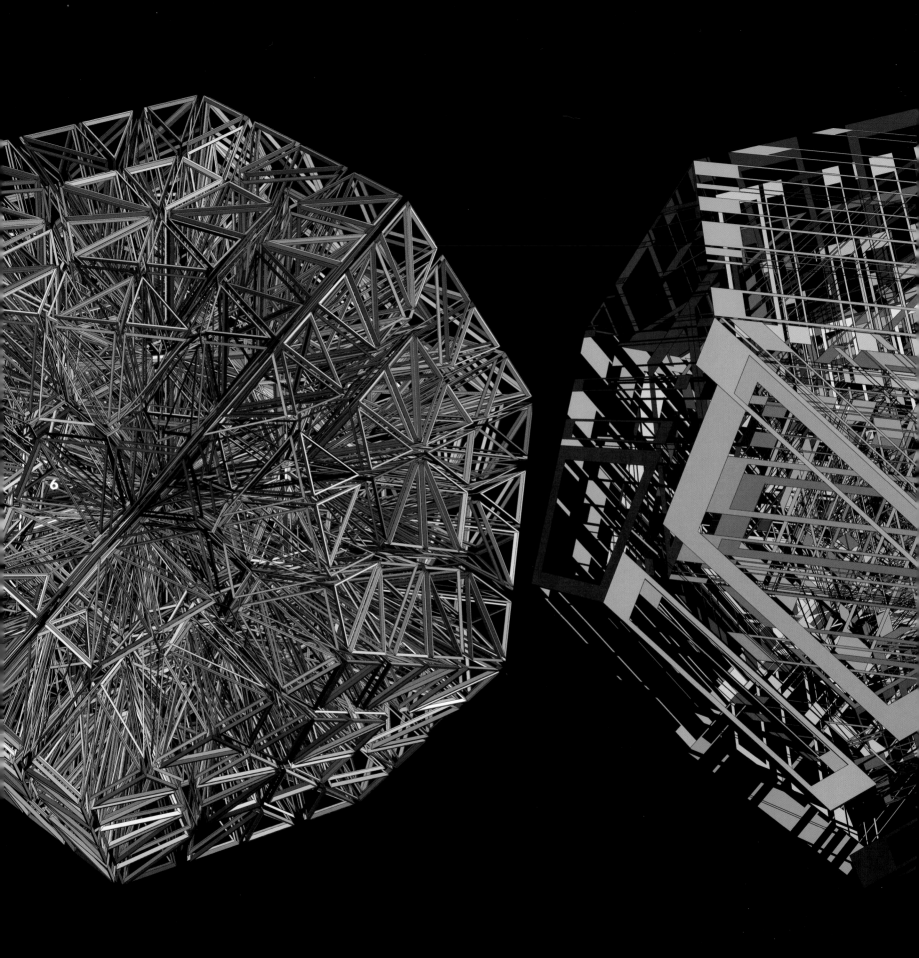

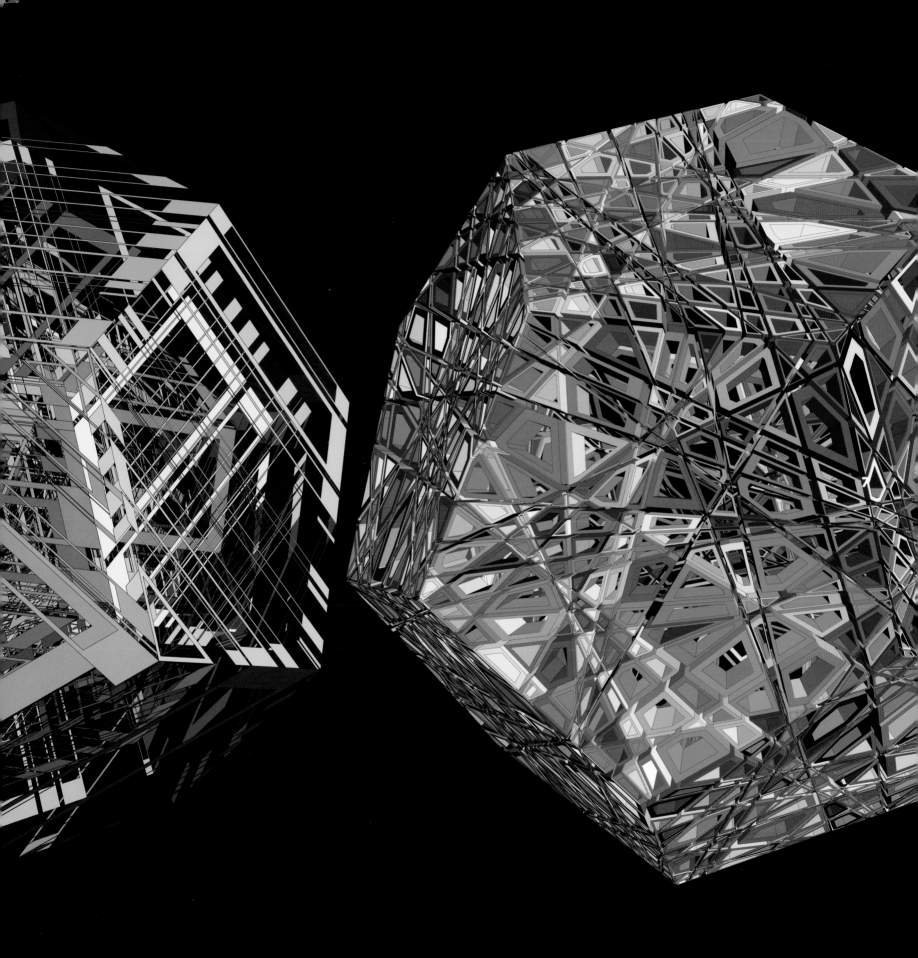

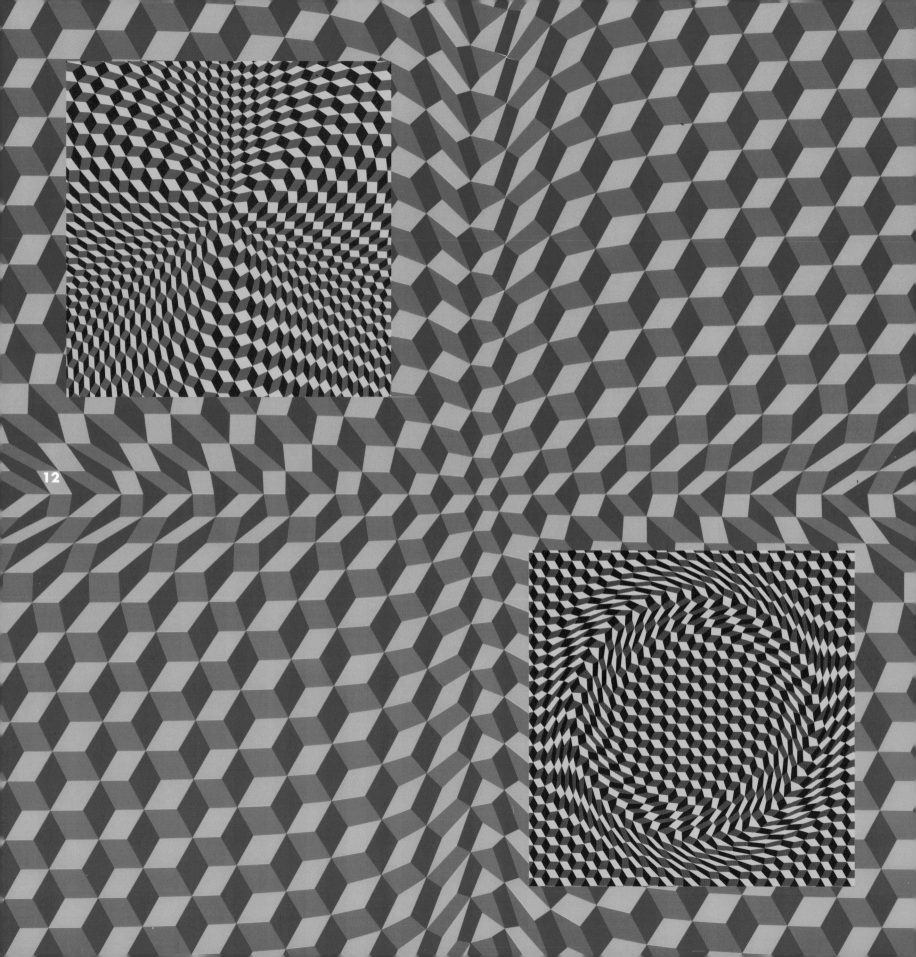

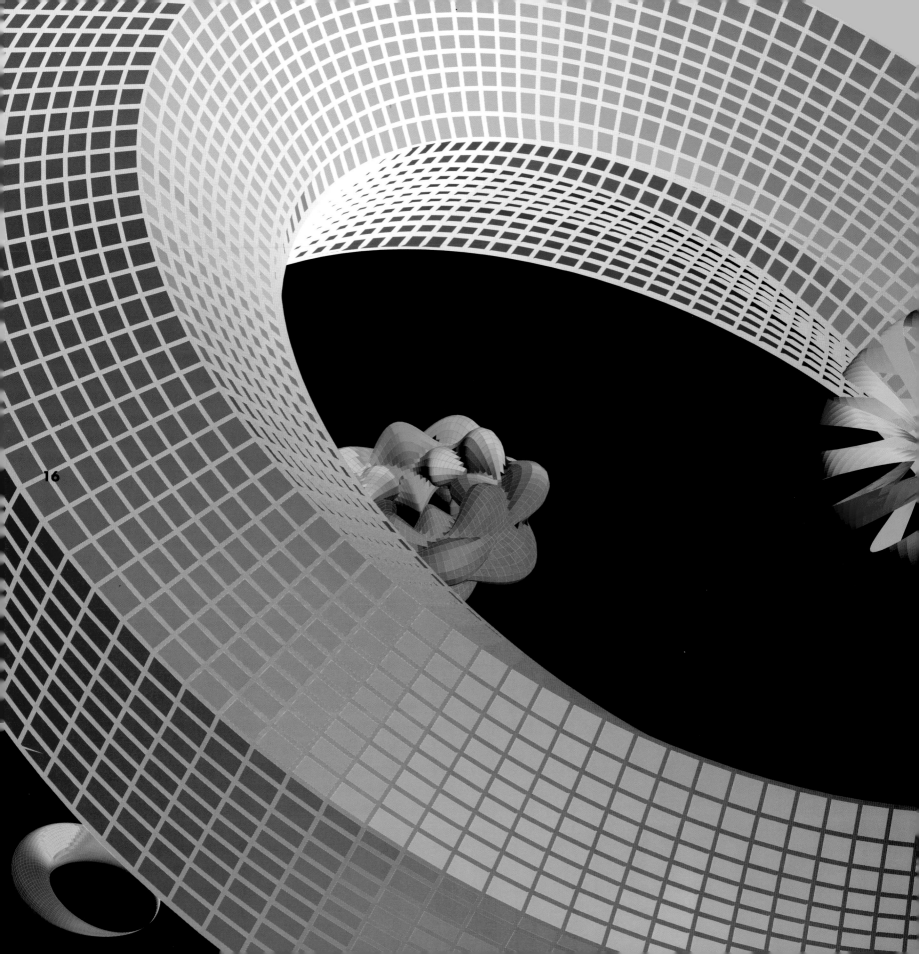

16

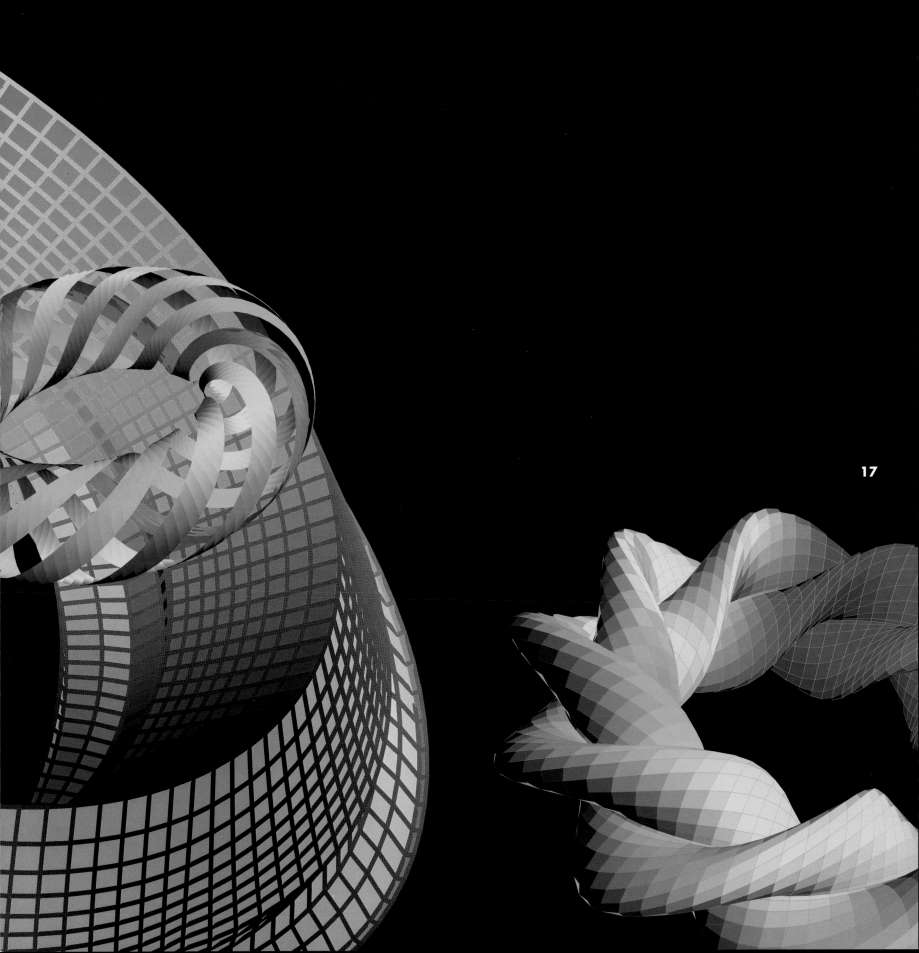

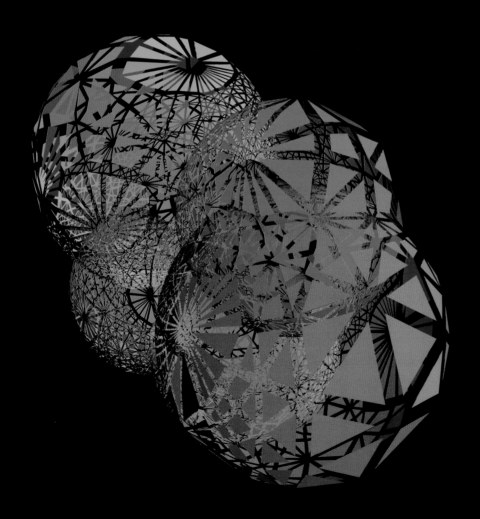

19

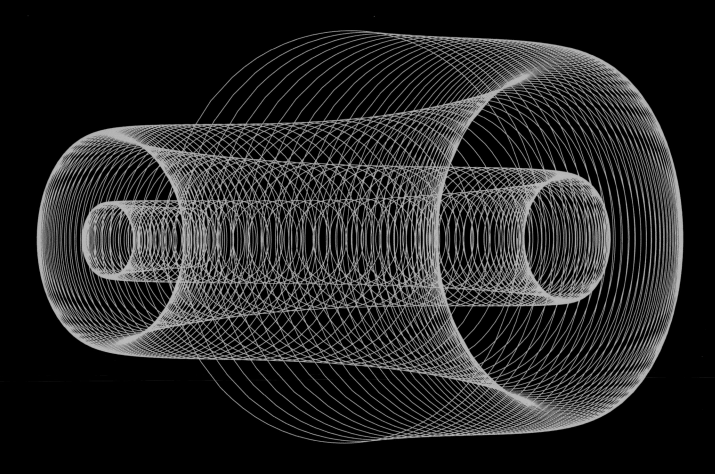

22

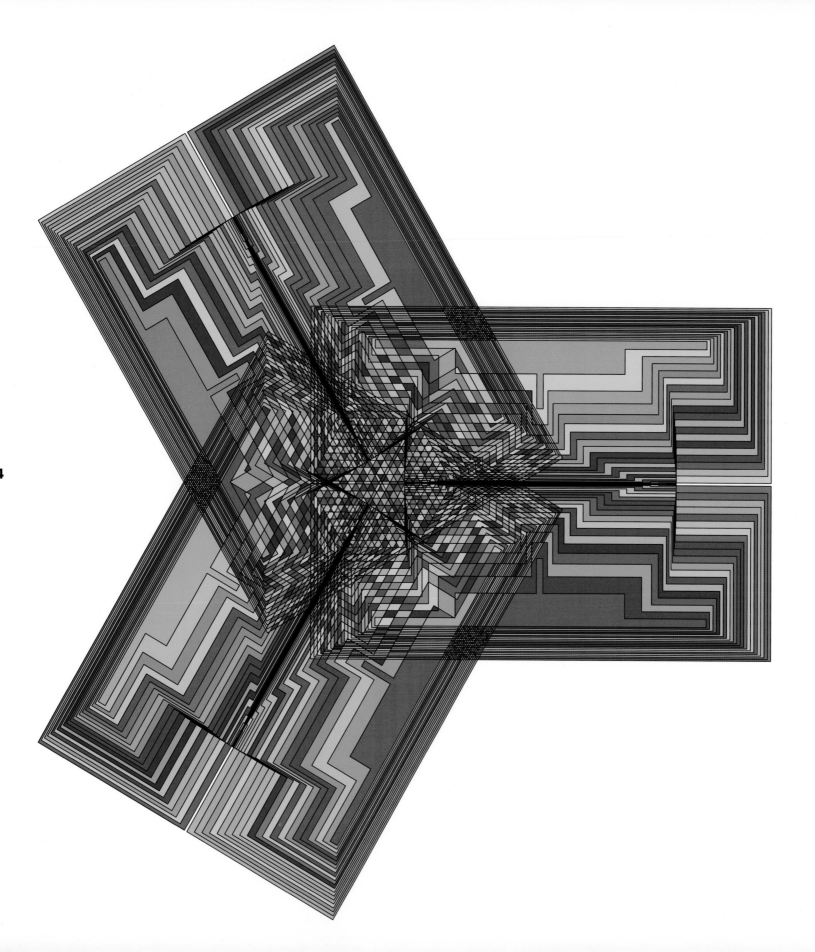

24

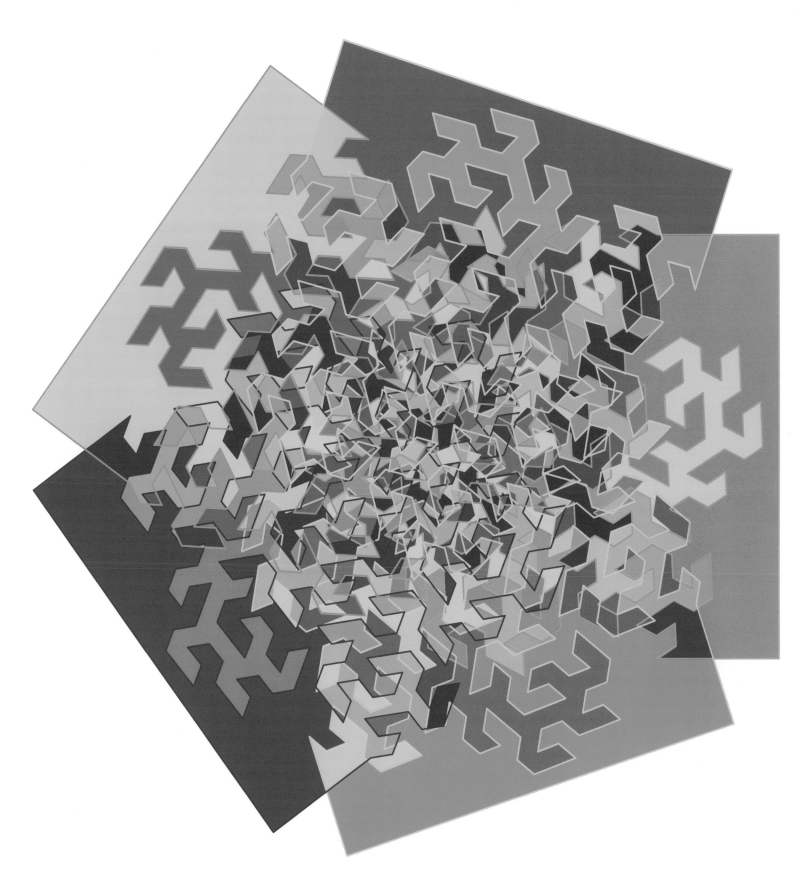

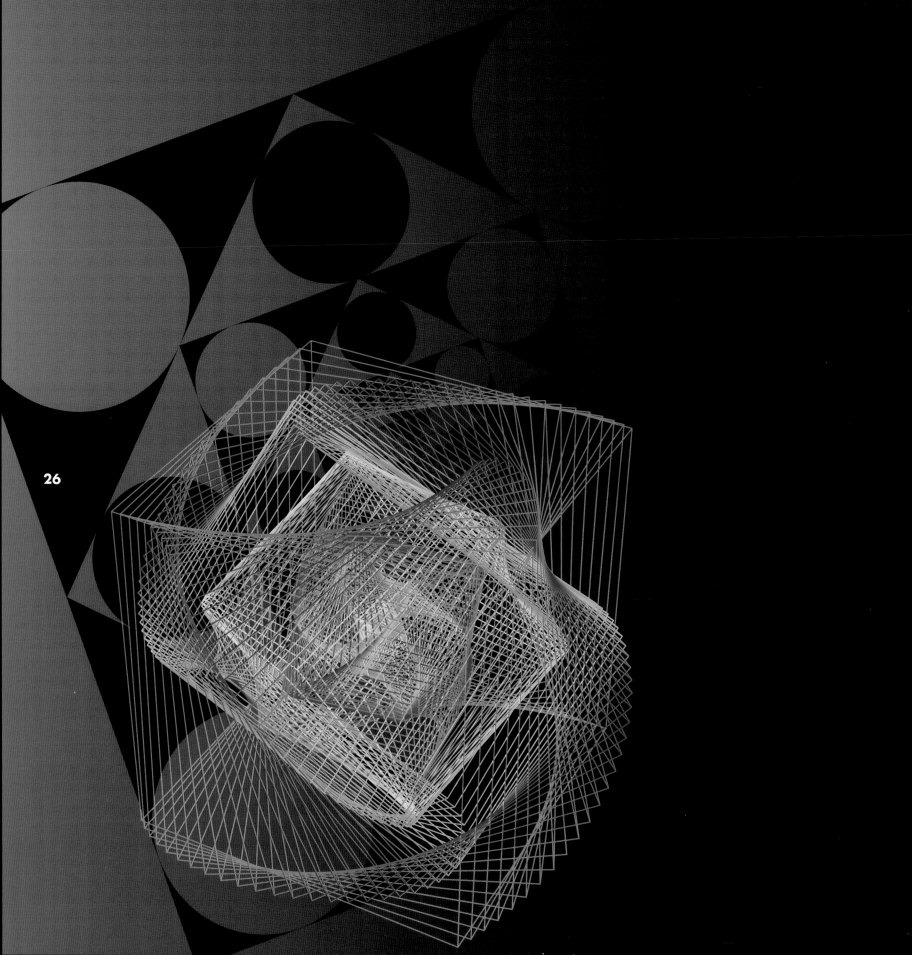

26

30

31

32

33

34

38

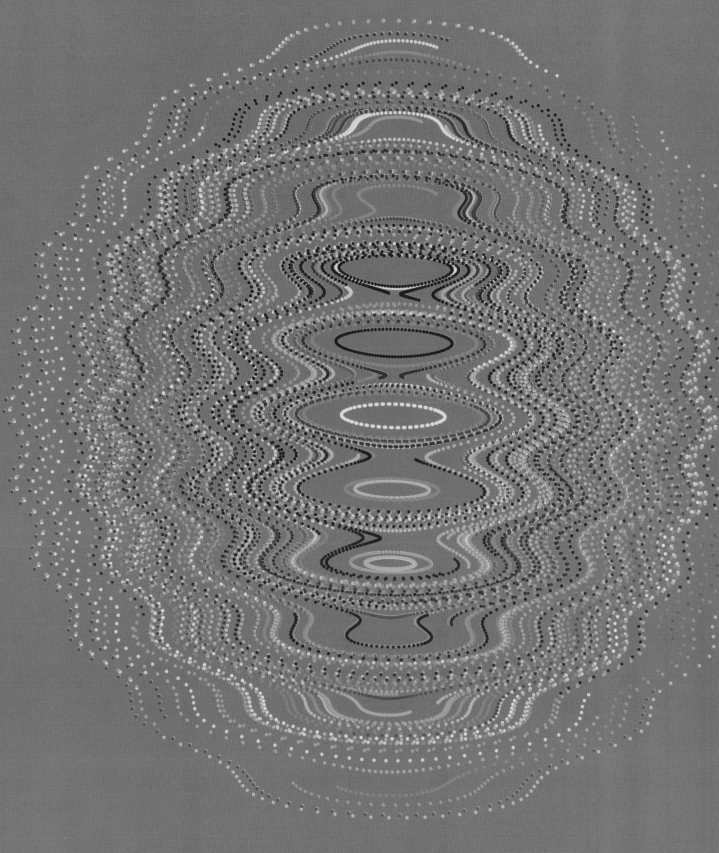

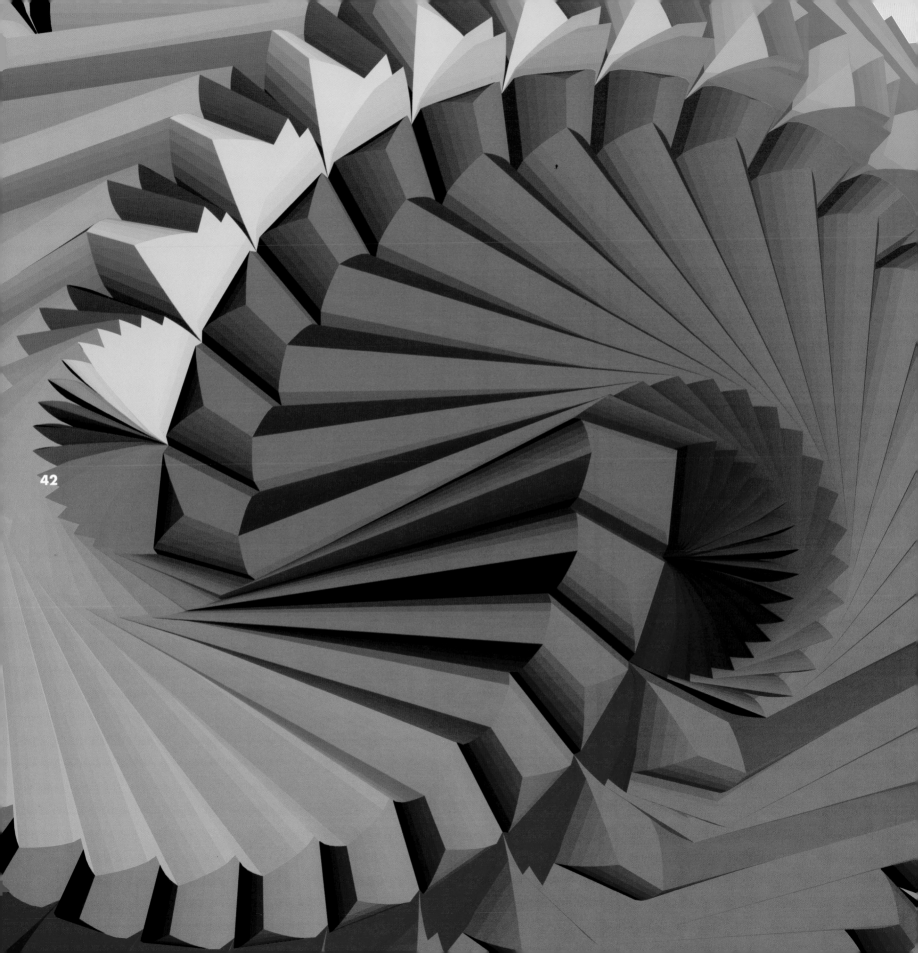
42

43

44

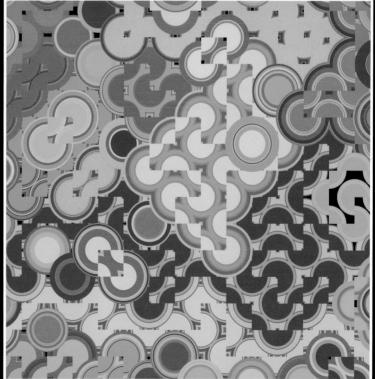

48

49

50

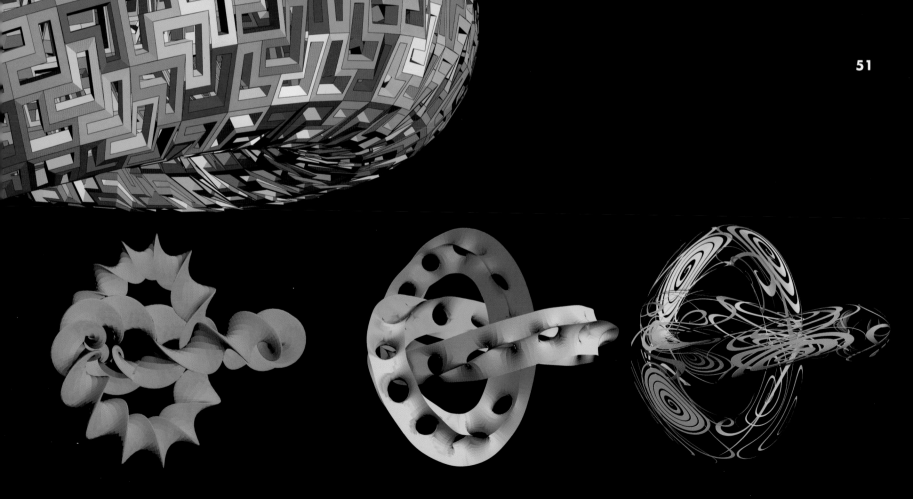

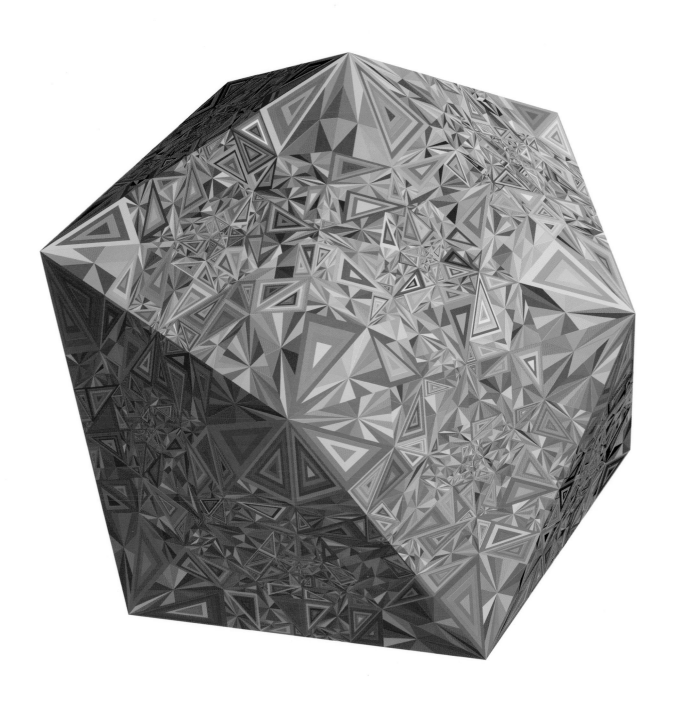

53

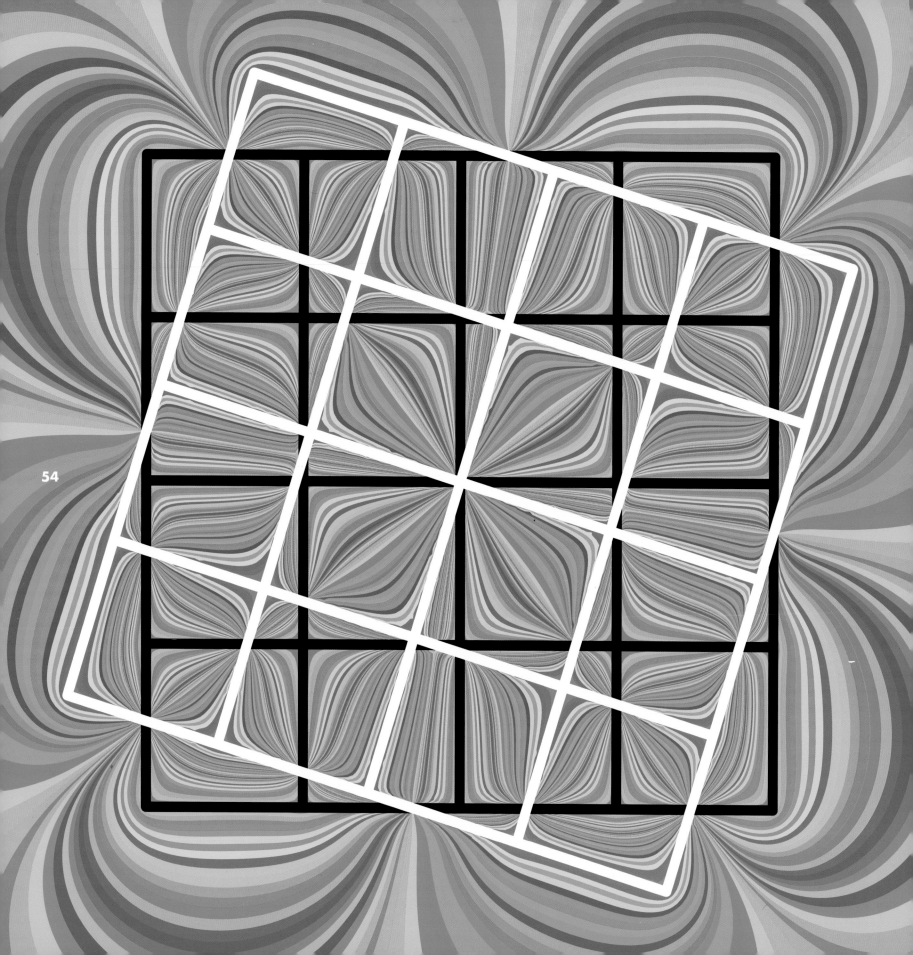

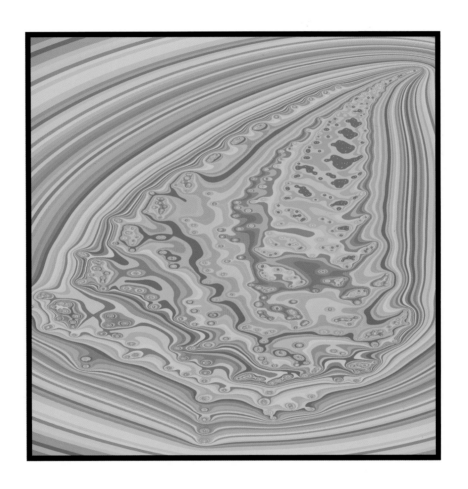

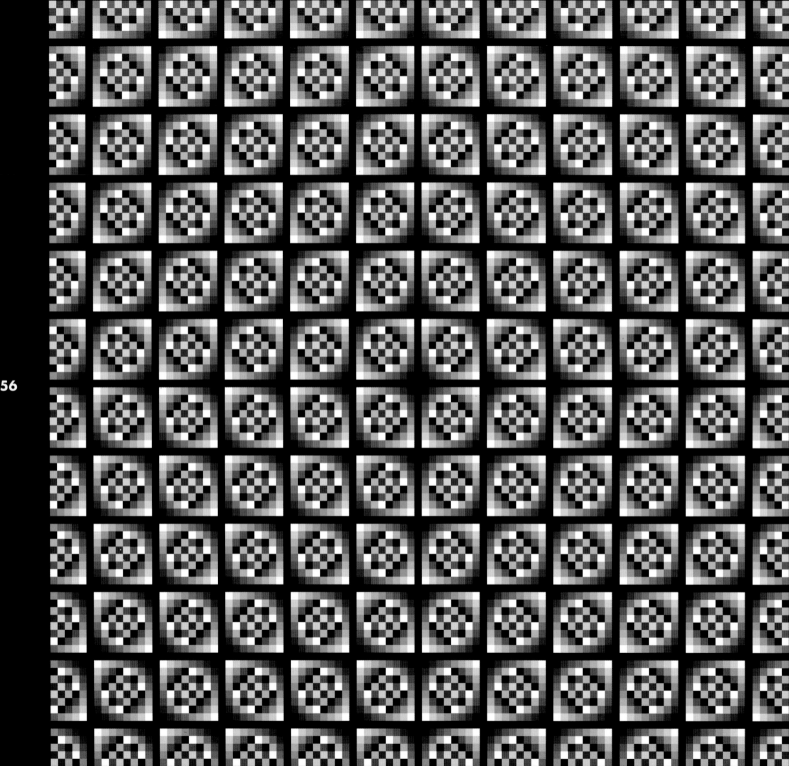

57

58

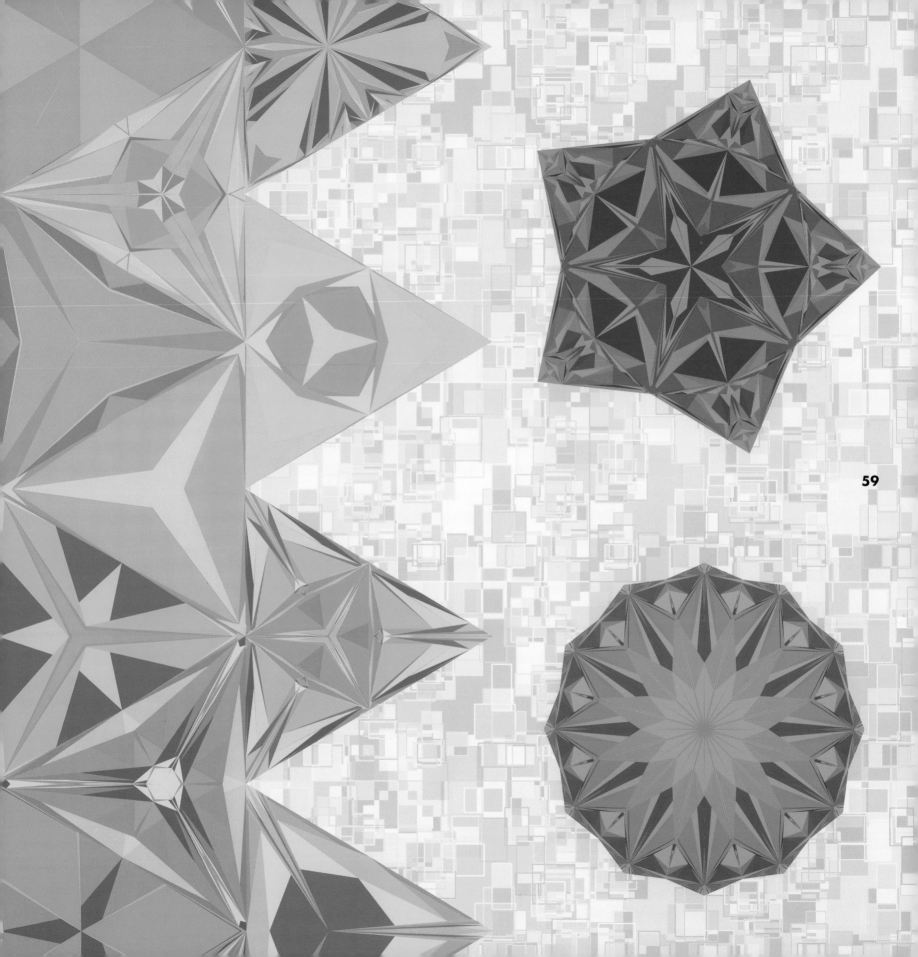

60

61

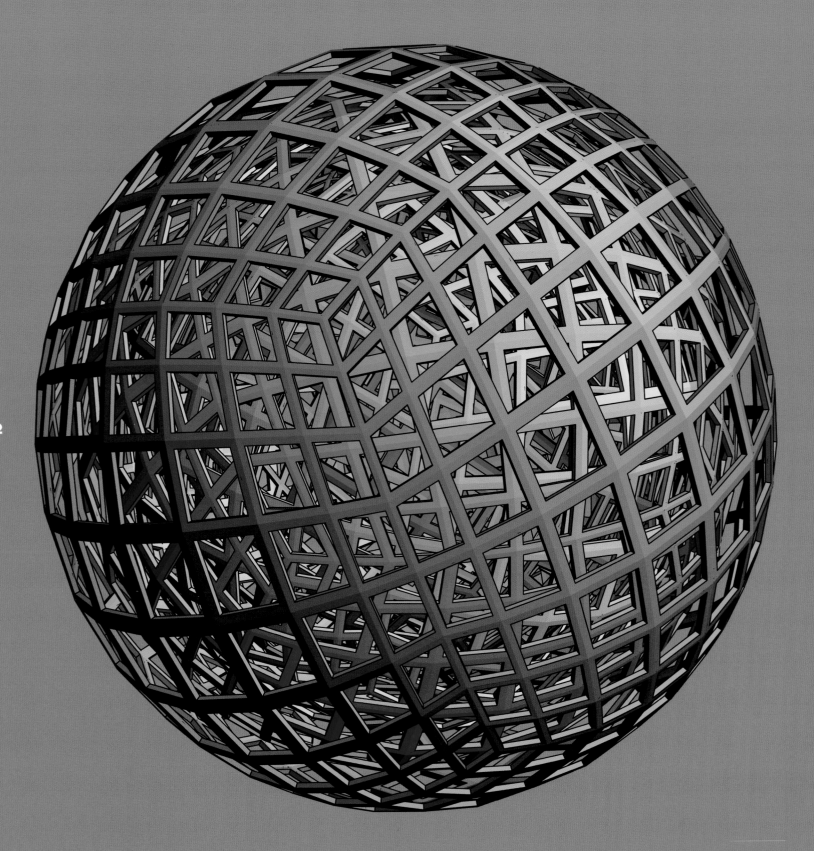

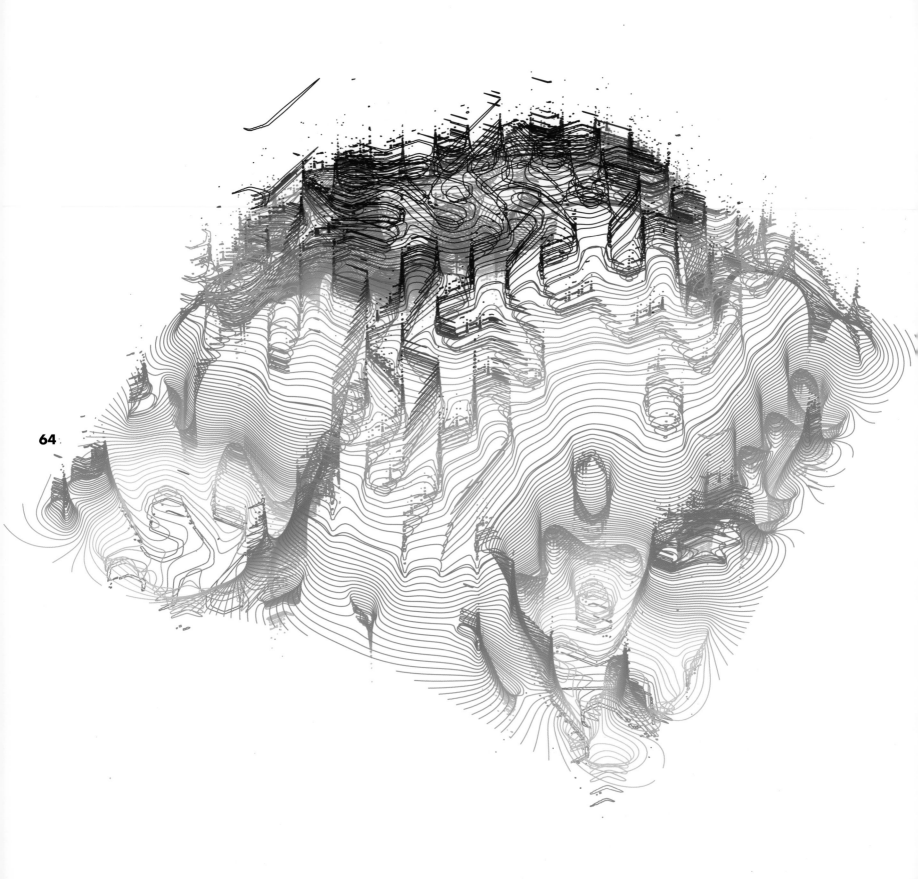

64

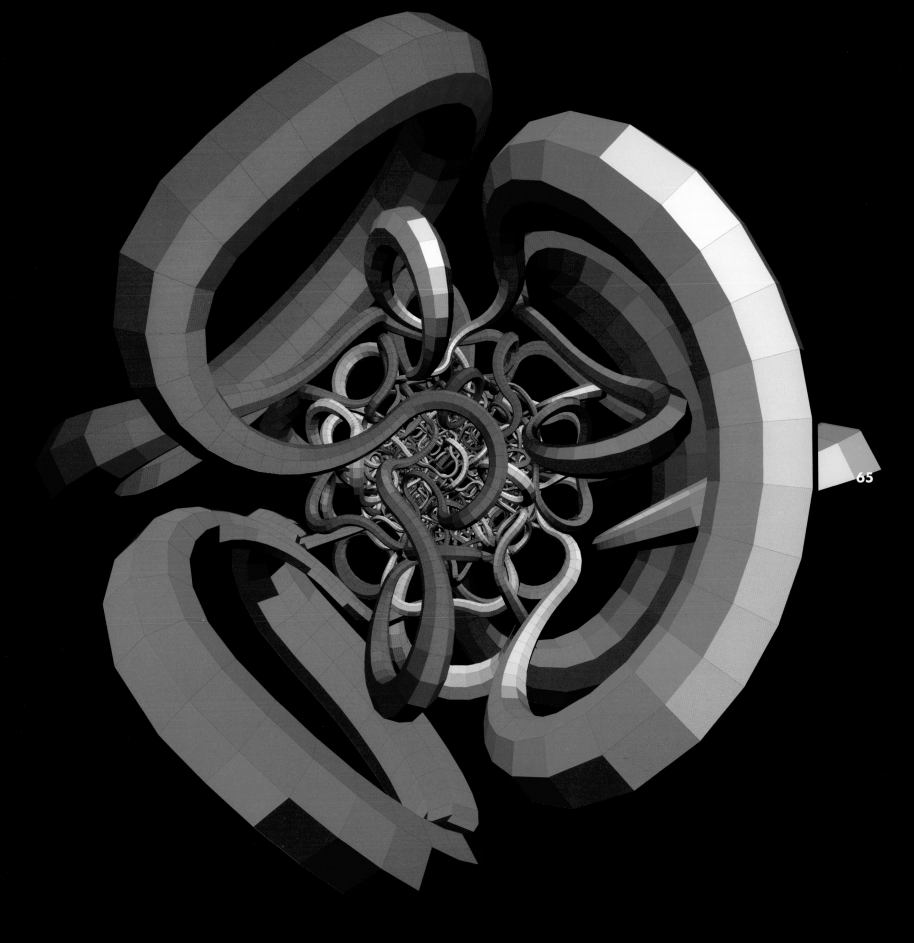

65

66

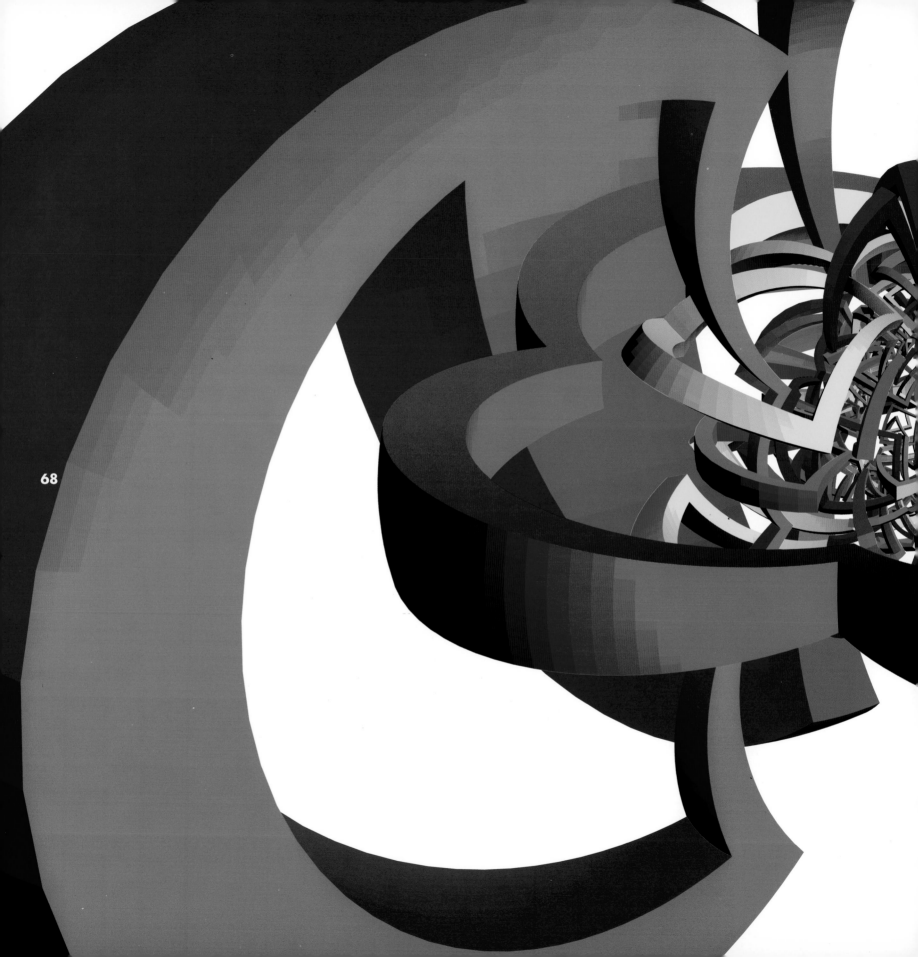

68

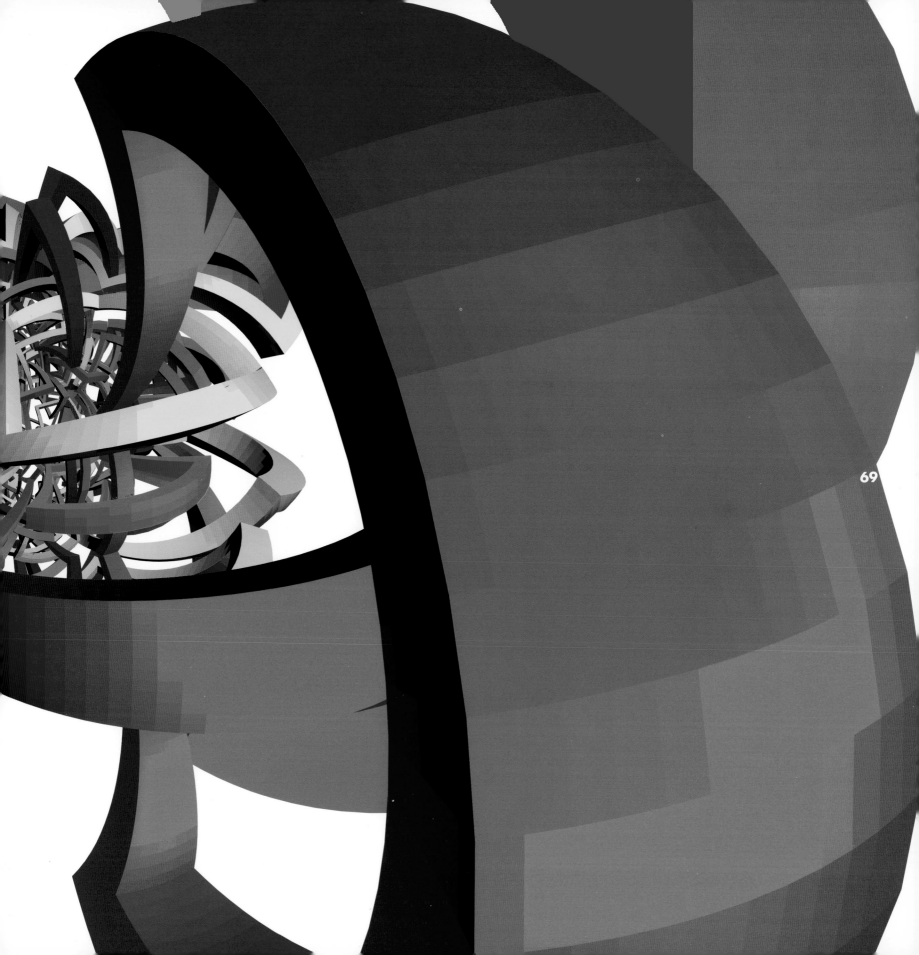

69

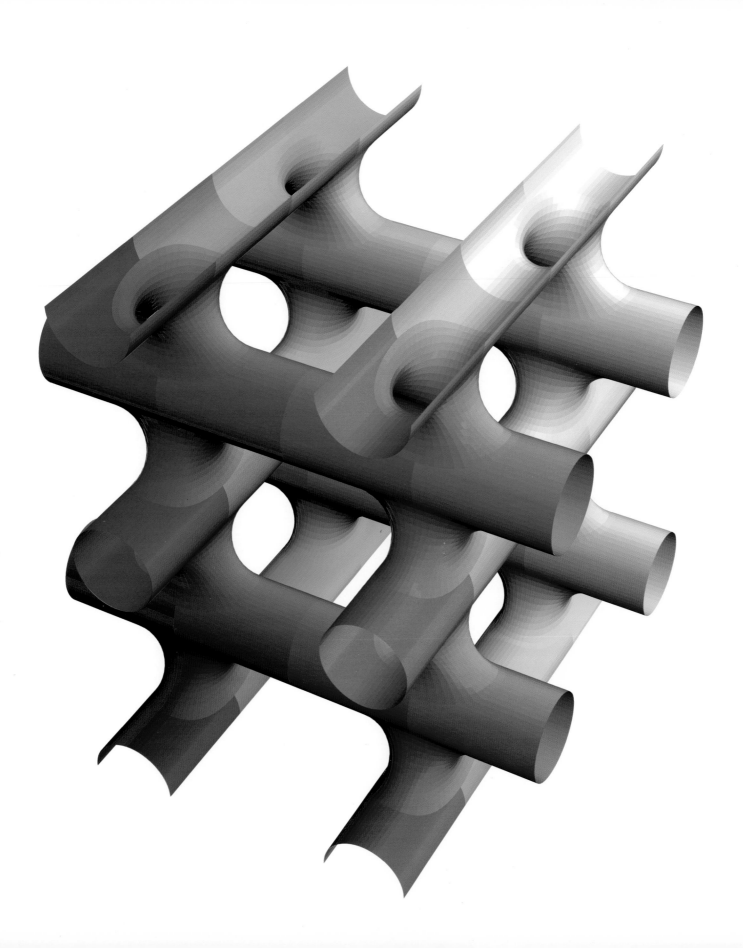

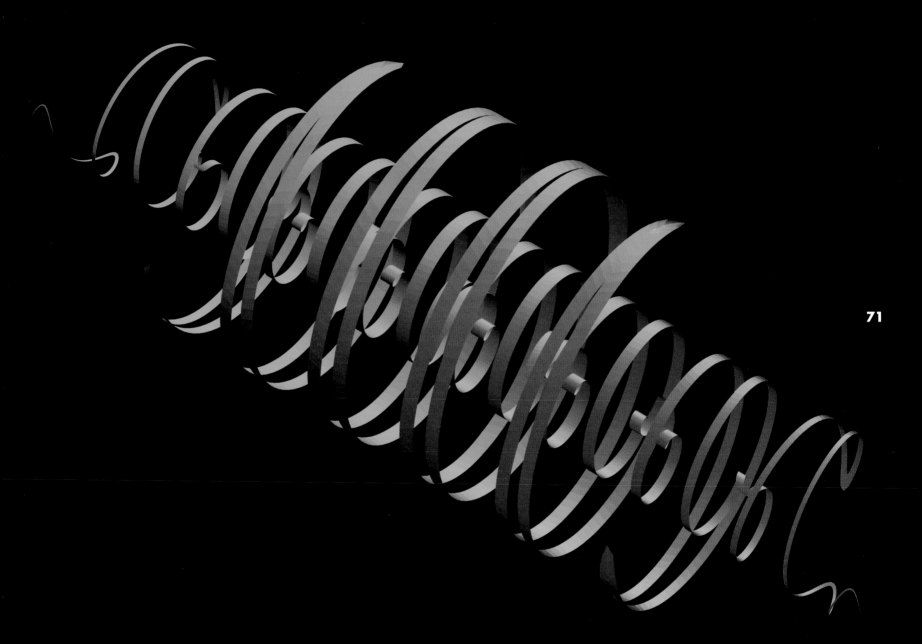

71

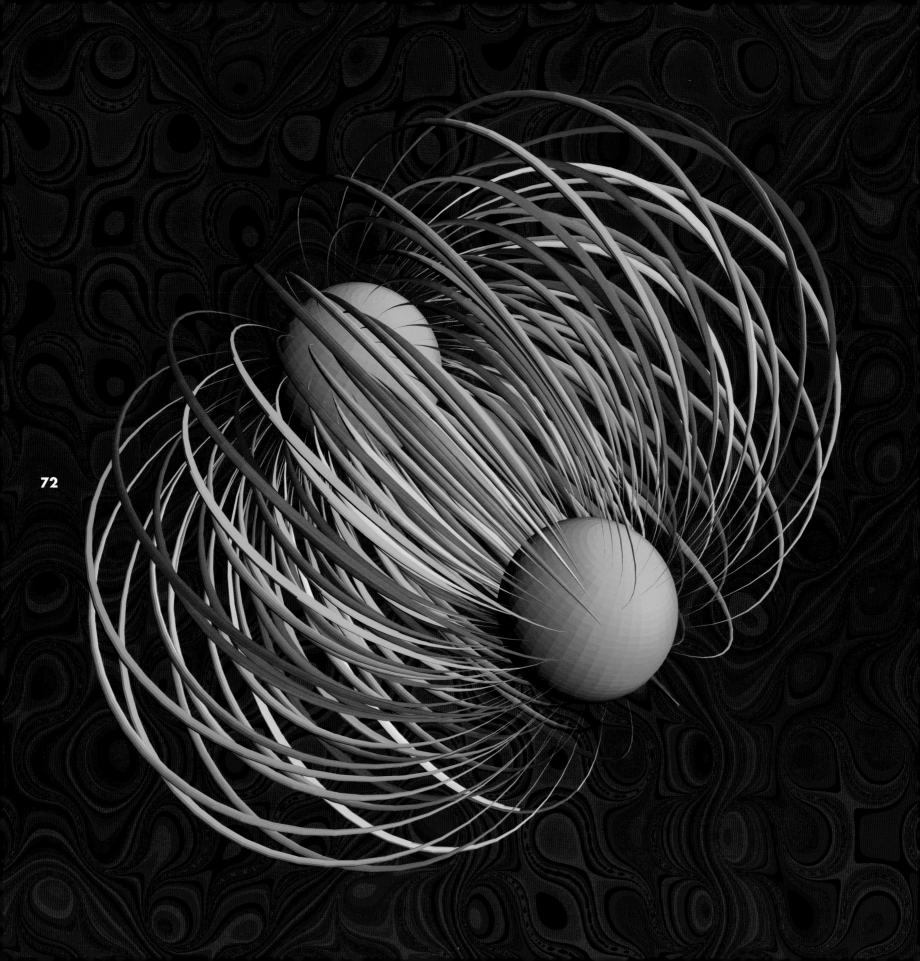

72

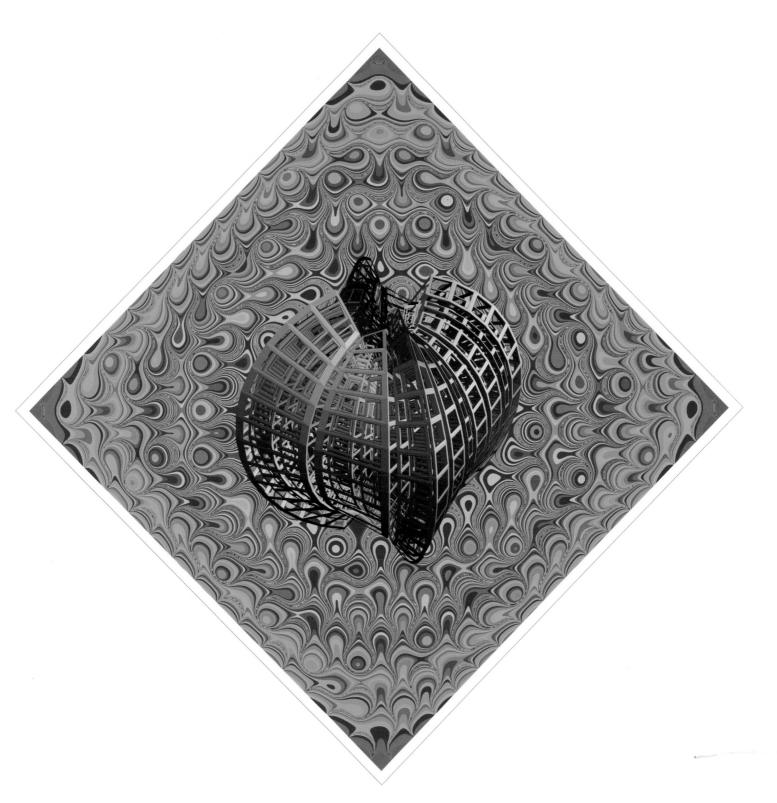

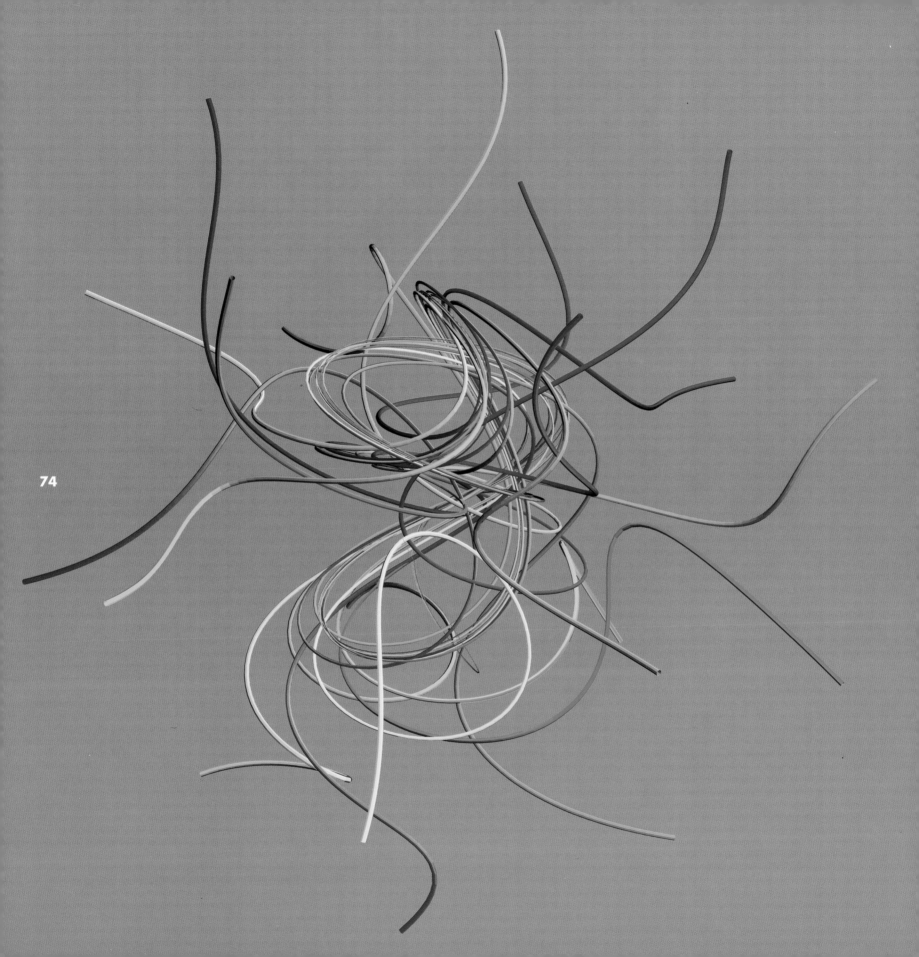

74

STEP BY STEP

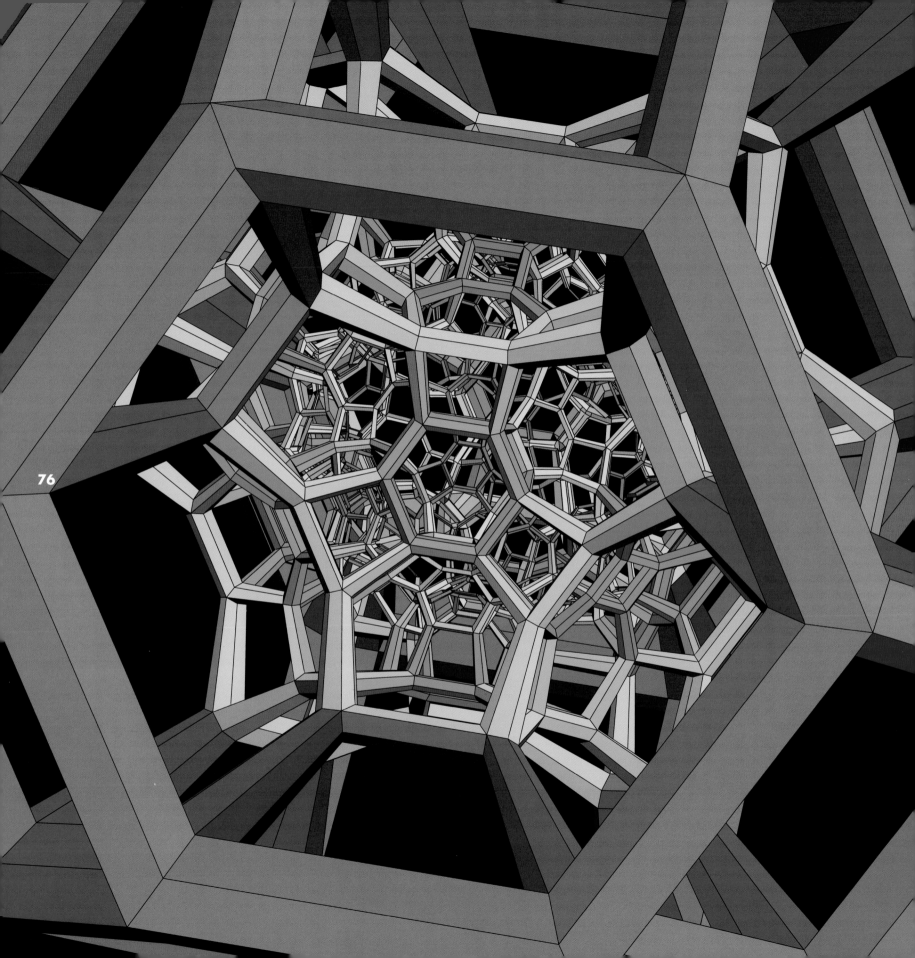
76

To accompany this gallery of *Mathematica* images, I felt it might be informative to describe, in detail, how I have used *Mathematica* in the creation of a particular image. The example on the left is an inverted lattice of orthotetrakaidecahedrons. Despite that imposing name, the concepts behind this graphic are not all that difficult. The recipe for this image has two basic parts: first, create a regular lattice by repeating a certain shape; second, turn that lattice inside out.

We begin by creating that basic shape, the orthotetrakaidecahedron or truncated octahedron. The *Mathematica* package **Graphics`Polyhedra`** contains definitions of the five Platonic solids. Here is an octahedron, made from eight equilateral triangles.

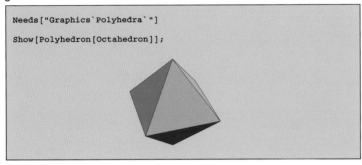

```
Needs["Graphics`Polyhedra`"]

Show[Polyhedron[Octahedron]];
```

If we then shave the vertices away to a certain level, using the function **Truncate**, the resulting shape is the orthotetrakaidecahedron. Each orthotetrakaidecahedron has six square faces and eight hexagonal ones for a total of fourteen; the "tetrakaideca" in the polyhedron's name means "fourteen." (It's also possible to create an orthotetra-kaidecahedron by starting with a cube and shaving away its eight corners.)

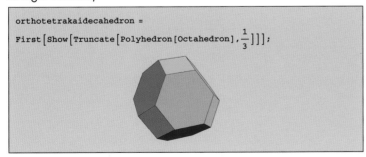

```
orthotetrakaidecahedron =
First[Show[Truncate[Polyhedron[Octahedron], 1/3]]];
```

Orthotetrakaidecahedrons are space fillers—that is, if you have many copies of the same shape at the same size, they can be packed together like a three-dimensional jigsaw puzzle, without any spaces between them. In this packing, each square face is pressed against a square face on another orthotetrakaidecahedron; the same is true of the hexagonal faces. That fact allows us to build up a cluster of orthotetrakaidecahedrons by creating a reflected polyhedron on each face. The function **mirror** reflects the polyhedron body on the plane formed by the polygon face. The function **midPoint** calculates the geometrical midpoint of a polygon or a polyhedron formed by polygons by averaging them.

```
midPoint[Polygon[points_]] := Apply[Plus, points]
                              ------------------------
                                   Length[points]

midPoint[polys : {_Polygon..}] :=
   Apply[Plus, Map[midPoint, polys]]
   ---------------------------------
           Length[polys]

mirror[body_, face_Polygon] :=
With[{μ = midPoint[face]}, Map[2 μ - #&, body, {-2}]];
```

We can generate a cluster of orthotetrakaidecahedrons, layer by layer, by performing this reflection on each of the starting polyhedron's faces and then repeating the operation on each successive layer. To remove duplicates, we keep a list containing the midpoints of the polyhedra we have generated previously. Before adding a new polyhedron to our cluster, we compare its midpoint against this list to ensure we aren't duplicating one we already have. Note that we don't have to create the entire polyhedron and then average the midpoints of its faces in order to know what its midpoint would be. It's faster to use the function **predictMidPoint** to simply determine where the first polyhedron's midpoint will be reflected.

```
predictMidPoint[body_, face_Polygon] :=
   2 midPoint[face] - midPoint[body]
```

These supporting functions, **mirror** and **predictMidPoint**, allow us to create a function named **mirrorBody** to actually carry out the reflection of the polyhedron into previously empty locations.

```
mirrorBody[body_] :=
With[{ε = 0.001},
Flatten[
   Function[μ, If[Min[#.#& /@ (μ - #& /@ midPointList)] > ε,
      AppendTo[midPointList, μ]; mirror[body, #], {}]][
         predictMidPoint[body, #]]& /@ body]
```

Starting with the orthotetrakaidecahedron defined above, which is assumed to have its midpoint on the origin, we can use **mirrorBody** to calculate increasing layers around our original polyhedron. The function **orthotetrakaidecahedronCluster** returns a list of the first *n* layers. (Incidentally, it's my *Mathematica* convention to avoid all but the most common abbreviations when naming functions, and I should warn you that the function names will become longer still.)

```
orthotetrakaidecahedronCluster [n_] :=
  orthotetrakaidecahedronCluster [n] =
    (midPointList = {{0, 0, 0}};
     NestList [Flatten [mirrorBody /@ #, 1]&,
       {orthotetrakaidecahedron}, n])
```

Here is our first layer of orthotetrakaidecahedrons.

```
Show [Graphics3D [orthotetrakaidecahedronCluster [1]]];
```

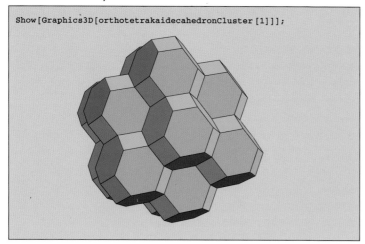

To look inside this cluster, we can delete the faces and simply look at the edges. To make the edges easier to see—as well as more interesting visually—we can also replace them with solid beams. This process is implemented via the routine **makeBeams**, which generates a beamed version of the polyhedra.

```
makeBeams [body_List, α_, β_] :=
With [{midPointBody = midPoint [body]},
  Function [1, Function [midPointPolygon,
   Apply [Polygon [
        {midPointPolygon + α (#1 – midPointPolygon),
              midPointBody + β (#1 – midPointBody),
            midPointBody + β (#2 – midPointBody),
              midPointPolygon + α
          (#2 – midPointPolygon) }]&,
    Partition [Append [1, First [1]], 2, 1], {1}]][
    midPoint [Polygon [1]]]] /@ Map [First, body]]
```

That gives us the following view.

```
Show [Graphics3D [beamedOrthotetrakaidecahedronCluster =
    Map [makeBeams [#, 0.85, 0.9]&,
      orthotetrakaidecahedronCluster [1], {2}]]];
```

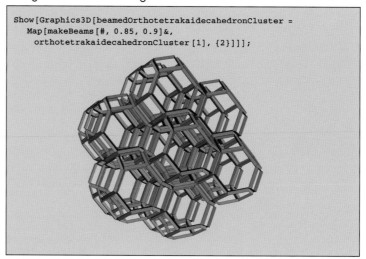

We can then assign a hue to each beam according to its distance from the origin.

```
norm [vector_List] := √‾vector . vector‾

Show [Graphics3D [{EdgeForm [Thickness [0.0001]],
    {Hue [0.15 norm [midPoint [#]]], #}& /@
     Flatten [beamedOrthotetrakaidecahedronCluster ]}],
   Lighting → False];
```

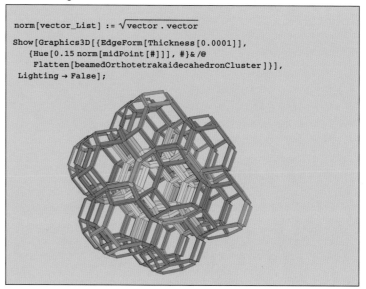

The last step is to turn this object inside out. We can do this by transforming every point $\vec{r}$ of the polygons in the last picture into the point $\vec{r}/r^2$ where r is the point's distance from the center of the central polyhedron. This transformation moves the detailed structure inside the central orthotetrakaidecahedron. The viewpoint has been chosen to give the best view of the internal structure.

```
inversion[graphics_] :=
  graphics /. Polygon[l_] ⊗ Polygon[#/#.#&/@1]

Show[inversion[%%], PlotRange → All,
  ViewPoint → {2, 3, 4}];
```

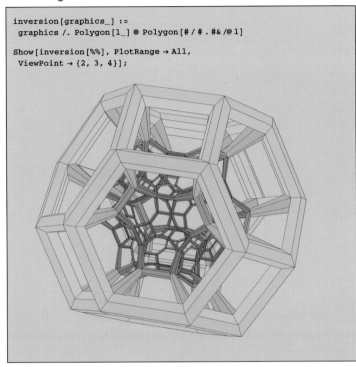

Combining all the steps together in one function, named **InvertedOrthotetrakaidecahedronLattice,** gives us the following.

```
InvertedOrthotetrakaidecahedronLattice [
  ω_Integer ? Positive, color_, opts___] :=
Module [
 {beamedOrthotetrakaidecahedronCluster , α = 0.85, β = 0.9},
beamedOrthotetrakaidecahedronCluster =
  Map[makeBeams [#, α, β]&,
    orthotetrakaidecahedronCluster [ω], {2}];
Show[inversion[Graphics3D [{EdgeForm[Thickness [0.0001]],
    {color[norm[midPoint [#]]], #}&/@ .
      Flatten[beamedOrthotetrakaidecahedronCluster ]}]],
  opts,
  PlotRange → All, ViewPoint → {2, 3, 4}]]
```

This function, with a different coloring, produces the final form to be used in the image.

```
InvertedOrthotetrakaidecahedronLattice [2,
  SurfaceColor[Hue[1 - #/4], Hue[1 - #/4], 2]&;
```

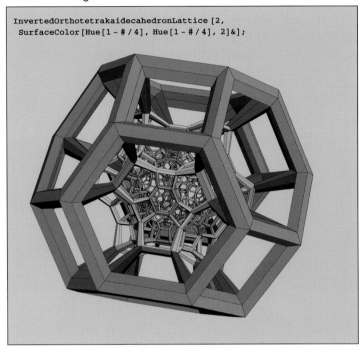

On page 76 you will find—cropped and with a different background color—the result of generating two layers of polyhedra with **InvertedOrthotetrakaidecahedronLattice**.

79

VISUAL INDEX

Note: The principles used to create many images in this gallery are quite simple. However, the mathematical tools used to create a number of others are comparatively arcane and likely to be unfamiliar to anyone without a graduate degree in math or physics. A complete explanation of concepts like Brillouin zones or Truchet patterns would be, to borrow the common textbook phrase, beyond the scope of the present work. For more information on such topics, see Michael Trott's *The Mathematica Guidebook* (TELOS/Springer-Verlag, 1999).

82

End paper

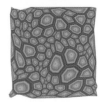

Contour plot, with only three contour values, of a random superposition of trigonometric functions.

Cover

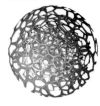

Delauney triangulation on nested half spheres.

Front matter

Colored Delauney triangulation of a randomly selected set of points within a unit square.

Spread 2–3

Three-dimensional mosaic formed by slicing a cube with 70 randomly chosen planes and then slightly shrinking each fragment.

Contour plot of a low-order piecewise-continuous interpolation of random data on a square grid.

Nested perforated cubes. The cubes' faces are of finite thickness, and a spherical volume is subtracted from each cube.

Cube in which faces are divided using the t_essela_tion featured in Escher's print *QuadratLimit*.

Worn stones. A cubic lattice of randomly distorted spheres.

Cmutov surface. The surface $(8x^4 - 8x^2 + 1) + (8y^4 - 8y^2 + 1) + (8z^4 - 8z^2 + 1) = 0$

Spread 4–5

Islamic decorative pattern mapped onto a sphere.

Random tesselation of the surface of a sphere. Each piece has been expanded outward slightly.

Colored 3D Hilbert curve mapped into a sphere.

Horn-shaped spirals opening along the directions of the faces of a dodecahedron.

Tesselation of the unit disk induced by the set of points $\exp(i(5^i \bmod 257))$ projected onto a sphere.

Arcs of circles spliced together in such a way that the resulting curve is smooth.

Spread 6–7

Dodecahedron sliced by 100 randomly chosen planes. The resulting fragments are shrunk slightly.

Nested arrangement of dodecahedra with faces sliced by families of parallel planes. Each remaining polyhedron is then perforated.

A dodecahedron subdivided into 120 tetrahedra, each of which is recursively subdivided into 9 more tetrahedra.

Spread 8–9

The faces of a Platonic solid are triangulated, and then randomly chosen triangles are rotated outward or inward along the edges of the Platonic solid. The path each triangle sweeps out is marked by a series of polygons.

Parallel sets of lines chosen with a normal Gaussian probability along the edges of a square lattice.

Spread 10–11

Asteroids made from tangential lines on a square lattice. This technique was among the first used in computer art.

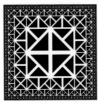

Tesselation of a square as featured in Escher's print *QuadratLimit.*

Hyperbolic tesselation of a disk, similar to that featured in Escher's print *Circle Limit IV (Heaven and Hell).*

Graduated rotation of a circular region of a square lattice.

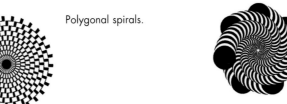

Polygonal spirals.

Truchet-like pattern on a square lattice. Note that this pattern is built from only two fundamental square tile designs.

Recursive staggered triangles.

Vasarely-like view on a ball with squares.

Brillouin zones of a 2D hexagonal lattice.

Contour plot of Chebychev polynomials U_n.

83

Rotated and progressively enlarged black and white disks.

Pinecone-like pattern of polygons arranged along radial spirals.

Chebychev polynomials T_n wrapped around successive circles.

Filled Gosper curve.

Bands wrapped around a torus.

Spread 12–13

Distorted array of Kepler cubes à la Grignani.

Islamic ornamental pattern.

Torus-like figure with cross section distorted in a periodic fashion.

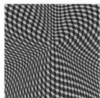

Distorted array of Kepler cubes with threefold symmetry.

Square divided into two regions by a Peano curve.

Torus-like figure whose cross section interpolates smoothly between a triangle, a square, a pentagon, and a hexagon.

Distorted array of Kepler cubes with sixfold symmetry.

Spread 14–15

Random arrangement of colored spirals.

Dupin cycloid.

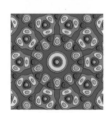

Contour plot of a random sum of trigonometric functions with 10-fold rotational symmetry.

Random arrangement of colored sine waves.

Spread 18–19

Inverted ($\vec{r} \longrightarrow \frac{\vec{r}}{r^2}$) higher order Brillouin zones of a cubic body-centered lattice.

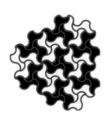

Periodic arrangement of identical shapes after Cundy.

Spread 16–17

Torus-like figure with elliptical cross section. The cross section is rotated as one travels along the main circle.

Individual polygons of a randomly chosen plane of the Brillouin zones of a 3D cubic face-centered lattice.

Spread 20–21

Recursive inversions ($\vec{r} \longrightarrow \frac{\vec{r}}{r^2}$) starting with a set of five circles.

Five overlaid Gosper curves, with the resulting polygonal regions assigned random colors.

Random pieces of spirals overlaid, with polygonal regions assigned randomly selected colors.

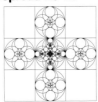

Extended phase portrait of a nonlinear 2D oscillator.

Spread 26–27

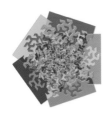

Recursive arrangement of black and white disks in shrinking squares.

Spread 30–31

The faces of a Platonic solid simultaneously extended radially, rotated randomly, and shrunk.

Spread 22–23

Random arrangements of 3D polygons projected into 2D and then subdivided, mirrored, and rotated.

Recursive arrangement of black and white disks in shrinking triangles.

The faces of a dodecahedron simultaneously extended radially and shrunk.

Contour plot of a random superposition of functions with radial and azimuthal symmetry.

Randomly rotated and shrunk edges of a cube.

Smooth surfaces connecting the center and the vertices of a dodecahedron.

Rigid interwoven Chernoff frames.

Edges of a tetrahedron rotated outward until they again form a tetrahedron.

Spread 32–33

The faces of an icosahedron simultaneously rotated outward and shrunk.

Spread 24–25

Six overlaid series of concentric polygonal curves, with the resulting polygonal regions assigned random colors.

Spread 28–29

Random pieces of spirals overlaid, with polygonal regions colored alternately black and white.

The faces of two icosahedra simultaneously rotated outward and shrunk.

85

Twisted torus made from a chain built from the transformed icosahedron discussed previously.

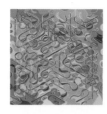

Equipotential plot of a placement of discrete charged pieces along the arcs of a hexagonal Truchet pattern.

Spread 42–43

Extruded Voderberg polygons forming a Voderberg spiral with tiles colored according to position along the spiral arms. The spiral is then projected onto a sphere.

Spread 34–35

Polygonal structures form the faces of platonic solids, and similar polygonal structures connect each adjacent pair of faces.

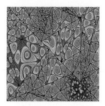

Equipotential plot of points forming a random tesselation of the plane into triangles.

Extruded Voderberg polygons forming a Voderberg spiral with tiles colored randomly.

Spread 36–37

Rectangular array of circles progressively enlarged and rotated randomly.

Equipotential plot of randomly charged pieces along a hexagonal Truchet pattern.

Extruded and perforated versions of Voderberg polygons forming a Voderberg spiral with tiles colored randomly.

86

Rectangular array of circles progressively enlarged and rotated randomly. Additional circles are transformed into astroid-like shapes to fill the spaces between the disks.

Equipotential plot of charged circles and triangles.

Randomly colored Voderberg polygons arranged in a spiral.

Spread 38–39

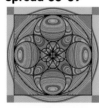

Contour plot of the function $f(x,y) = \prod \text{circles}(x,y)$, where the product ranges over a set of iteratively inverted circles.

Equipotential plot of four iterations of the Koch snowflake given alternating charge.

Spread 44–45

Colored bands following the closed and open curves of Truchet patterns.

Spread 40–41

Iterated points of a stochastic web formed by
$$x_{i+1} = \sin(\alpha)y_i + \cos(\alpha)(x_i + \beta \sin(2\pi y_i))$$
$$y_{i+1} = \sin(\alpha)y_i + \sin(\alpha)(x_i + \beta \sin(2\pi y_i))$$
for randomly chosen values for α and β.

Equipotential plot drawn with many more contour lines than potential data. The data describes randomly charged pieces of a hexagonal Truchet pattern.

Spread 46–47

Various Lindenmayer systems, due to Prusinkiewicz and Lindenmayer modeling herbs and grasses.

A collection of curves repeatedly bifurcated and extended. Each curve is continuous, and all share a common starting segment.

The finite part of the Scherk minimal surface $\sin(z) = \sinh(x) \sinh(y)$ mapped along a trefoil knot.

Spread 56–57

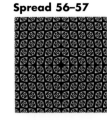

Density plot of a matrix arising in a quantum mechanical eigenvalue problem.

Barnsley's fern, a well-known fractal image created by the iterated application of four affine maps.

Three segments of tube rotated along a trefoil knot in such a way that the result is a single long tube.

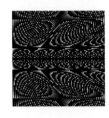

Saunders picture of a^b in base 3.

Spread 48–49

Various transformations applied to the mouse from the German ARD-TV program *Die Sendung mit der Maus*.

Spread 52–53

An Easter egg. The faces of an icosahedron were randomly subdivided, and the resulting polygons were projected onto an egg-shaped surface of revolution.

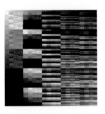

Density plot of a matrix arising in a quantum mechanical eigenvalue problem.

Spread 50–51

The surface of a trefoil knot covered with nonperiodic tiling. The pattern is developed by recursively subdividing one L-shaped region into four smaller ones, each L-shaped.

The faces of an icosahedron, randomly subdivided and assigned random colors.

Density plot of the multiplication table of a finite group.

87

A tube with its cross section distorted in a periodic manner, shaped into a trefoil knot.

Spread 54–55

Equipotential plot of two square lattices given opposite charge.

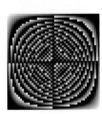

Density plot of $x\,y \bmod n$, where $n = 50$.

A tube with a rotating ellipse for a cross section, shaped into a trefoil knot.

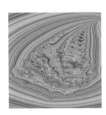

Equipotential plot of a field created by arranging charged points in the shape of a Barnsley fern.

Density plot of a matrix reflected iteratively along its edges.

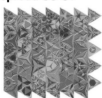

Randomly generated symmetric polygonal patterns.

Randomly generated symmetric polygonal patterns.

Random colors assigned to regions created by randomly positioning overlapping squares.

Randomly generated symmetric polygonal pattern.

Randomly generated symmetric polygonal pattern.

88

Traces of a set of points randomly rotated and moved toward a central point.

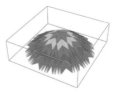

Paths of a set of nearly parallel light rays inside a reflecting quartic surface.

Contour plot of the function $\sum z^{n^2}$ near the boundary of the unit disk.

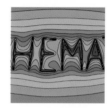

Zeros of the partial sums of the series of $\exp(z)$.

Rotated and braided tubes.

Beginning with a random concave polygon, the points that initially point inward are reflected outward until a convex polygon is finally formed.

Recursive solution of the so-called Apollonian problem, finding a circle tangent to three other circles; each circle is defined in turn by its three largest neighbors.

Cusp made from recursively subdivided polygons.

Faces of a dodecahedron evenly subdivided and given a checkerboard coloring.

Contour plot of the potential field formed by charging the letters of "Mathematica."

Five tori glued together by manipulating their implicit polynomial representation.

Floating 3D "A"s.

Kepler's recursive subdivision of the pentagon.

An assortment of Platonic solids scaled to share the same edge length and glued together edge-to-edge.

Colored version of Hofstadter's butterfly, the energy spectrum of a quantum mechanical particle in a periodic potential and a magnetic field.

Spread 62–63

Riemann surface of the algebraic function $w(z)^4 = \sqrt{z^2 - 1}$.

Nested spheres obtained by subdividing the faces of a cube and projecting them onto a sphere.

Spread 64–65

Offset 3D contour lines of a charged hexagonal Truchet pattern.

Inversion ($\vec{r} \longrightarrow \frac{\vec{r}}{r^2}$) of a 3D cubic Truchet pattern of interlocking tubes.

Spread 66–67

Contour plot of the real part of the function `InverseEllipticNomeQ`. This is a modular function that is analytic within the unit circle. There is a dense set of singularities along the unit circle.

Set of superposition movements of circles on circles.

Spread 68–69

Inversion ($\vec{r} \longrightarrow \frac{\vec{r}}{r^2}$) of a 3D array of interlocking square structures.

Spread 70–71

Sets of connected parallel tubes, with junctures smoothed using the ball blending method.

A plot of the 2D curve $y(x) = \frac{\sin(x)}{x^2 + 1}$ is widened, and then the plane upon which the curve is drawn on is "rolled" parametrically.

Page 72–73

Field lines between two spheres with equal but opposite charge.

A randomly generated 2D Peano curve is extruded along a cylinder; the resulting cylinder is then mapped onto a sphere.

Equipotential plot of a charged hexagonal Truchet pattern.

Page 74

Paths swept out by a random set of points moving toward a single guiding point, which is also in motion.

89